Regu

Regulative Dentification Conference

28.10.95

Psychic Experience
and Problems of Technique

Harold Stewart, a distinguished psychoanalyst of more than 30 years' experience, began his medical career as a general practitioner. He was drawn first towards hypnotherapy, then to psychoanalysis, as a more sensitive, productive and far-reaching method of exploring patients' problems.

In this book Dr Stewart draws deeply on his own clinical experience to focus on changes in the patient's experience of inner space, and to record the growth of his own understanding of the patient's experience and how this can change. Beginning with a vivid account of the role of collusion in the myth of Jocasta and Oedipus, he goes on to a theoretical discussion of thinking, dreams, inner space, and the hypnotic state, in the context of extensive clinical experience. The second part of the book centres on practical clinical issues and problems of technique, tackling in particular the role of transference interpretations, other agents of change, and the problems encountered in benign and malignant types of regression.

The wealth of clinical material and the author's informality and openness in presenting his experiences of working with very disturbed patients will be of immense practical value to other practitioners. *Psychic Experience and Problems of Technique* will help psychoanalysts and psychotherapists to understand the nature of clinical problems which are often encountered but seldom acknowledged.

The New Library of Psychoanalysis was launched in 1987 in association with the Institute of Psycho-Analysis, London. Its purpose is to facilitate a greater and more widespread appreciation of what psychoanalysis is really about and to provide a forum for increasing mutual understanding between psychoanalysts and those working in other disciplines such as history, linguistics, literature, medicine, philosophy, psychology, and the social sciences. It is intended that the titles selected for publication in the series should deepen and develop psychoanalytic thinking and technique, contribute to psychoanalysis from outside, or contribute to other disciplines from a psychoanalytical perspective.

The Institute, together with the British Psycho-Analytical Society, runs a low-fee psychoanalytic clinic, organizes lectures and scientific events concerned with psychoanalysis, publishes the *International Journal of Psycho-Analysis* and the *International Review of Psycho-Analysis*, and runs the only training course in the UK in psychoanalysis leading to membership of the International Psychoanalytical Association – the body which preserves internationally agreed standards of training, of professional entry, and of professional ethics and practice for psychoanalysis as initiated and developed by Sigmund Freud. Distinguished members of the Institute have included Michael Balint, Wilfred Bion, Ronald Fairbairn, Anna Freud, Ernest Jones, Melanie Klein, John Rickman, and Donald Winnicott.

Volumes 1–11 in the series have been prepared under the general editorship of David Tuckett, with Ronald Britton and Eglé Laufer as associate editors. Subsequent volumes are under the general editorship of Elizabeth Bott Spillius, with Christopher Bollas, David Taylor, and Rosine Jozef Perelberg as associate editors.

IN THE SAME SERIES

NEW LIBRARY OF PSYCHOANALYSIS

13

General editor: Elizabeth Bott Spillius

Psychic Experience and Problems of Technique

HAROLD STEWART

Foreword by Pearl King

TAVISTOCK/ROUTLEDGE
LONDON AND NEW YORK

First published in 1992
by Routledge
11 New Fetter Lane, London EC4P 4EE

Simultaneously published in the USA and Canada
by Routledge
a division of Routledge, Chapman and Hall Inc.
29 West 35th Street, New York, NY 10001

Typeset by LaserScript Limited, Mitcham, Surrey
Printed in Great Britain by Mackays of Chatham PLC, Chatham, Kent

British Library Cataloguing in Publication Data

Stewart, Harold *1924–*
Psychic experience and problems of technique. – (The
New Library of Psychoanalysis v 13).
1. Psychoanalysis
I. Title II. Series
150.195

Library of Congress Cataloging in Publication Data

Stewart, Harold, 1924–
Psychic experience and problems of technique/Harold Stewart,
p. cm. – (New library of psychoanalysis: 13)
1. Psychoanalysis. I. Title. II. Series.
RC504.S73 1991
616.89'17 – dc20   91-10695
CIP

ISBN 0–415–05974–7
0–415–05975–5 (pbk)

To Joy
for all her help,
patience, and forbearance

Contents

Foreword

PEARL KING

Harold Stewart, whom I have known and worked with for many years, has collected together and elaborated several of his papers around the topic of changes in the patient's experience of his inner space.

Harold Stewart has been a Training Psychoanalyst of the British Psycho-Analytical Society for many years and is Chairman of its Education Committee. In the tripartite division into groups in the British Society, he has been trained and has worked as a member of the 'Independent Group', which developed from the majority of the British Society in 1946. This Independent Group whose members were themselves firmly based in Freud's approach to psychoanalysis, were not considered to be members of Melanie Klein's Group or of Anna Freud's Group; nevertheless they have been ready to evaluate and make use of the work of colleagues like Melanie Klein and Anna Freud when their ideas seemed helpful in their work with patients.

The first part of the book emphasizes theoretical issues, but these are presented within the context of extensive clinical material. The book has an autobiographical flavour and the reader will be aware that the author is taking him or her into his consulting room as he struggles to understand and work with his patients, sharing his increasing knowledge of psychoanalysis, interwoven with his own growing experience as a psychiatrist and psychoanalyst. Following his qualification in medicine, Harold Stewart became a General Practitioner. The influence of this early professional experience comes through to me in his sensitivity to his patients as whole persons rather than as a series of symptoms or a metapsychological construct. In his attempt as a GP to understand the psychological problems of his patients, he became fascinated with the problem of how to understand what had gone wrong with patients who were psychosomatically ill or had been psychically damaged, and what needed to take place in order that therapeutic change and psychic growth could occur. He became interested in hypnotherapy as an approach to their problems.

The first chapter describes his discovery of the limits of hypnotherapy, and the reasons why he was drawn towards psychoanalysis in order to be in a position to explore these problems further. His interest in hypnotherapy drew his attention to the role of collusion in relationships and mental illness, and his discussion of the Greek myth of Jocasta and Oedipus in the second chapter explores collusive mechanisms at work in a literary setting, from which it is easy to see clinical parallels.

In the next three chapters dealing with 'Changes in Inner Experience' he discusses the experience of dreaming and its relation to the 'transference' and illustrates it with very sensitive clinical material. His classification of different types of dreams is useful, particularly his delineation of 'ego-distancing dreams' and 'ego-overwhelming dreams'. Many patients these days seek psychotherapeutic help on account of feelings of 'inner emptiness' and inability to feel 'real'. The patient whom he describes complained of having an 'empty space' inside her which was very persecuting to her. She was not however aware of not being able to feel real until the end of her analysis, when she became able to experience 'real space'. He compares his patient with the description given by Marion Milner of her patient in her book, *The Hands of the Living God*. He links 'inner space' which is experienced as 'empty space' with 'schizoid emptiness', and 'real space' with 'depressive emptiness' which alone can lead to 'positive emptiness'. He discusses the contributions of other writers, including Winnicott and Grotstein, to this topic. Harold Stewart's interest then naturally turns to the function and understanding of the process of 'thinking' and he illustrates and describes three levels of the experiencing of thinking, again richly augmented with examples from his clinical work, and alongside a discussion of Bion's contribution to the study of thinking.

The second part of the book is concerned with technical issues and problems of effecting psychic change. Again these issues are discussed within the context of extensive clinical material. Being a product of the British Psycho-Analytical Society, Harold Stewart's approach to technique centres on the exploration of the patient's object relations and on interpretation of transference phenomena, rather than the analysis of resistances or the analysis of intersystemic conflicts.

In Chapter 6, 'Types of transference interpretation: an object-relations view', he describes his approach to the analysis of transference material, describing different ways of understanding transference within the context of an 'object-relations' approach to psychoanalytic technique. He describes how he incorporates analysis of resistances and conflicts within an object-relations approach. While he sometimes appears to treat as a transference manifestation any relationship or activity to which the patient may refer as referring to himself, regardless of its link to the patient's past (which is a current fashion in the British Society), he is also critical of this approach and of a slavish use of Strachey's so-called 'mutative interpretation' as the only path to therapeutic change. In the last chapter, 'Interpretation and other agents for psychic change', he explores and discusses the therapeutic value of various types of communication that take place between the analyst and his patient, and their importance as agents for psychic change.

In Chapter 7, 'Problems of management and communication', Harold Stewart discusses the many management problems that can develop during the analysis of very disturbed borderline and psychotic patients or those suffering from gross hysteria, a discussion which will be of help and encouragement to many therapists, for such problems as he describes are often encountered but seldom acknowledged. In his clinical material, in addition to describing the difficulty of maintaining and protecting the psychoanalytical situation he spells out his conceptual hypotheses concerning each phase in the analysis of the patient, and the rationale for his responses and interpretations. Of particular interest to me was a phase in which one of his patients felt she could only communicate to herself and to her analyst through her paintings, and the way he made use of them, following the work of Marion Milner.

It is generally accepted that the psychoanalytic method of treatment and the context of the psychoanalytic situation facilitates and even encourages in the patient some degree of regression to earlier developmental experiences, whether it is in terms of affects, memories, bodily perceptions and needs, impulses, anxieties, defences against fears or wishes. Some analysts have attempted to facilitate and even to manipulate this process of regression by actively encouraging their patients to regress. Harold Stewart discusses this problem, emphasizing both the dangers of active encouragement of regressive episodes and the acting-out that can follow, and also the importance of being able to recognize and interpret within the analytic relationship. He gives a useful survey of the literature on the subject and his description of Michael Balint's contribution is very clear, including the differentiation that Balint makes between 'benign regression' and 'malignant regression'. He adds his own contribution to understanding the problems that arise when an analyst is faced with a patient in a malignant regression, and it is here that he says that he relies on his counter-transference as a guide. He poses the question, how much does the analyst's own technique contribute to the development of a malignant regression in a patient? One might also ask how many analysts are even aware of this possibility.

All through the book, Harold Stewart is very much aware of his own affective reactions to the vicissitudes of transference phenomena during his work with patients, which, along with many of his colleagues in the British Society, he refers to as his 'counter-transference'. This term may be understood in various ways. The analyst's reactions and feelings may be a response to the way he is being treated or experienced by his patient as a transference figure from the patient's past, and the analyst may experience affects similar to those of the original figures from the patient's past; or there may be a reversal of transference roles, with the patient treating the analyst as he felt that he was treated as a child. On the other hand, the analyst may perhaps be reacting in terms of the original meaning of the term 'counter-transference'; namely, there may be an arousal in the analyst of a transference response to the patient related to the analyst's own unconscious needs which may be inappropriate and alien to his understanding of his patient at that moment. I have tried to spell out these differences because Harold Stewart's use of the term 'counter-transference' may not always be clear to those who use it in its original meaning. I myself increasingly use the term 'counter-transference' in its original meaning and find the additional use of the term 'counter-transference' to cover any affects which the analyst may have towards his patient confusing, so that I prefer to describe these as the analyst's 'affective response' to his patient's communications, which may turn out to have been evoked by the patient's transference or by the analyst's own counter-transference.

Harold Stewart has an easy style and he puts his ideas in such a way that laymen as well as psychoanalysts should be able to comprehend them and follow his arguments. He refers usefully to the work of other writers, not only psychoanalysts, and he draws on the literature in such a way as to make his work attractive to professionals outside his immediate circle. The topics and themes that interest him should also stimulate others working with patients, even though they may have a different approach to the treatment of mental illness.

Acknowledgements

My particular indebtedness is to Elizabeth Spillius, the present Editor of the New Library of Psychoanalysis for (1) asking me to convert my psychoanalytic papers into book form; (2) enabling me to discover something of which I had been unaware – that the differing papers, having emerged from the same mind, had more connections and interrelations than I had previously realized; and (3) her many valuable comments and suggestions on the draft text. I am also grateful to Eric Rayner for giving his time to read the draft and make helpful suggestions for improvements. Last, but not least, I am indebted to Helen Abbott, whose secretarial skills have enabled my hand-written copy to take professional shape.

Introduction

The world of psychic experience and the changes that can be observed to occur in it have long interested me. My early experiences in general practice with hypnotic techniques, and the problems associated with them, gave me some conviction of the need to recapture, if possible, the totality of an experience, real or phantasied, particularly where it had been psychically traumatic, in order for therapeutic change and psychic growth to develop in the patient. It is both the intellectual knowledge of experiences and the emotional states involved in them that need to be brought to conscious awareness for their assimilation and digestion into the main psychical stream.

After the initial successes that befall all beginners, I discovered the limitations of hypnotic techniques as a therapy, and like many of my predecessors, I was led on to psychoanalysis, where a new world of experience and understanding gradually unfolded before me. When seeking analysis, I had turned for practical advice to Michael Balint, since he was prominent in this country for his work in helping General Practitioners with their problems with patients, and had himself created and formulated the 'Balint Group' technique for training in this field. At that time, I had no conception of Freudian psychoanalysis being divided into three groups, now known as Contemporary Freudian, Independent, and Kleinian.

I chose as my analyst Dr Julius Rowley, a consultant psychiatrist at the Cassell Hospital, who was himself an analysand of Balint. This choice made me a member of the Independent Group, and overall, I have been satisfied with this outcome. I suspect, however, that if I had chosen otherwise, I would most probably have been equally satisfied, since the factors uniting the groups are far greater than those dividing them. Nevertheless, there would not then have been quite the same slant and orientation as that being presented in this book.

I have divided the subject-matter into two parts, Theory and Technique, with both grounded, apart from one chapter, in clinical

1

work and experience. The first section of Part One is devoted to two studies of collusive relationships. The first concerns my attempt to understand the reasons for changes that occur in the hypnotic state when the negative transference between patient and hypnotist is interpreted. It led to my realization of the collusive relationship that is an essential part of this state and my theoretical conceptualization of the underlying psychodynamics of the state. Following this, the second study, non-clinical, is one of the role of Jocasta in Sophocles' play, *Oedipus Rex*. It demonstrates the collusion between Jocasta and Oedipus in denying knowledge of many facets of their relationship, and I have postulated that in both the hypnotic state and the Greek tragedy, there is a collusive denial of hostile and destructive impulses and phantasies. These studies constituted my first psychoanalytical papers, both being of an applied nature, and I must leave a discreet blank on the unconscious motives for my choice of topics.

The second theory section concerns the changes that patients can feel in their own inner experience in specific areas. My interest in such changes in myself during the course of my own analysis alerted me to those that patients might describe to me, and this led to my speculations on the form and genesis of such changes, particularly in their relationship to transference issues. The chapters on changes in the experiencing of the dream, of inner space, and of aspects of thinking, are on such specific areas, and it is noticeable that these changes, which are intrapsychic in nature, arise in close combination with, and seem to follow, changes that have occurred in the transference–countertransference relationship, which is both an intrapsychic and an interpersonal phenomenon.

In my conceptualizing of both theoretical and technical issues, I find that it is firmly based on what I consider are two of the main characteristics of British psychoanalysis. These are the importance of object relationships and the importance of the here-and-now of the transference. Although I have not arrived at any overall statement or aim in my work, one thread that runs through it is the appreciation of the psychic experience of the patient, and of observing how it expresses itself in the vicissitudes of the analytic process, and of how it, itself, is affected by this process. The same considerations would also apply to the psychic experience of the analyst.

One aspect of this thread that is essential in analytic technique is the need for the analyst to be sure that he is taking in the patient's experience as best he can, and then ensure that he does not rush in to make interpretations. Too often, interpretations are not just based on the need to give the patient an understanding of the process at that moment, but rather on the analyst's need to feel he is being a 'proper' analyst, or else on his need to make interpretations that he feels would be acceptable to his colleagues. It is vital that the analyst should be capable of waiting in ignorance until things become clearer and until the patient has had a greater chance to find himself. I have been greatly influenced here by my experiences in my own analysis, my case supervision with Balint, and by the teachings of Donald Winnicott and Wilfred Bion; in addition I should add my other influential teachers, my patients.

In Part Two, the technical section of the book, the first chapter is an attempt to set out a brief classification of transference interpretations that can be made in the course of an analysis. It is largely based on the differentiation of the two types of object relationships made by Freud, the anaclitic and the narcissistic, and the clinical examples furnish illustrations of the transference. I need to describe briefly my use of the concept of the transference. It is not only being used in the classical sense as an inappropriate response to the analyst by the patient, as if it were based on the important object relationship from the patient's past. It also takes into account all interactions between the patient and analyst, with particular reference to the here-and-now, and also includes the living-out, the enactments in the analytic situation, of internal object relationships, which are assumed to be the complex resultants of the patient's past experiences, often distorted by projective and introjective identificatory mechanisms. This makes the transference concept considerably more complex, but it does seem to do more justice to the clinical experiences of the analytic situation, as is shown by much of the British writings on transference.

The major part of this section is devoted to the topic of therapeutic regression, which still remains a controversial issue. My aim, here, has been to examine the grounds of the controversy, particularly in the light of contemporary developments in the psychopathology and psychodynamics of the clinical phenomena encountered in severe regressions, which usually occur in severe hysterical states. I have noticed that when I write or talk on this subject, particularly of the experiencing by patients, during analysis, of early traumatic or phantasied events which previously they may never have experienced or thought of, some colleagues seem to believe that I have abandoned all concepts of defence analysis, of transference, of problems of covert or overt destructive attacks, and instead have entered into some sort of collusion with my patients. I am assumed to have gone back to the time of the early Freud, with the abreaction of unconscious traumatic experiences being the vehicle of therapeutic cure. The assumption is made that in my conceptual thinking, I have abandoned the developmental model of conflict and defence with primary internal and external objects, for one of deficiency and deprivation occasioned by bad relationships with primary external objects.

I think that part of the reason for this is that, although both of the two most important modern proponents of therapeutic regression, Balint and Winnicott, have both written of the need for the interpretive work that is essential in dealing with these states, neither has given much in the way of clinical illustrations of their work in this respect. In not giving sufficient weight in their examples to the more overt or covert destructive manifestations in these patients, they have, perhaps inadvertently, given the impression of a treatment, more by love and the experiencing of early states, rather than one based on the interpretation and understanding of the totality of the regressed experience in all its aspects. This is somewhat unfair, particularly to Winnicott, who repeatedly stressed the importance of destructiveness in achieving separation, individuation, and the state of concern, but nevertheless, both have underplayed it clinically. This omission has tended to reinforce Freud's negative attitude towards Ferenczi in this field, a topic more fully discussed in Chapter 8. I have attempted to rectify some of this in my clinical examples of the necessary interpretive work in Chapters 7 and 10.

In all my analytic work with patients, the basic model that I use for my analytic technique is of understanding and interpreting conflicts and defences in all their aspects in the transference–counter-transference relationship. Very occasionally, and only if appropriate, I use regressive experiences, in the ways that I describe later, for their authentic therapeutic effect.

Theory

1

Collusion and the hypnotic state[1]

My introduction to the therapy of emotional disorders occurred soon after my qualification as a doctor in 1947, when I took my first post as a House Physician at Oldham Royal Infirmary, a hospital in Lancashire. One of my chiefs was a local General Practitioner who was interested in therapeutic abreactive techniques in psychiatry, and one day he suggested that I might like to watch him abreacting a patient. She was an elderly woman and all I remember of her was that she could speak only in an incomprehensible babble. He injected a small dose of Pentothal, which put her into a light sleep, and then suggested to her that she would now speak clearly and he asked her to recite the nursery rhyme, 'Mary had a little lamb'. She did so very clearly and distinctly and we were both impressed by this. He then suggested to her that when she awoke, she would be able to speak clearly and normally, yet when she did awaken, she disappointed us by relapsing into babbling. In this experience, I learned of the power of unconscious resistance, of its circumvention by abreactive techniques, and the relative uselessness of direct simple suggestion.

Some time after this, I became a General Practitioner myself outside London and rapidly became acquainted with the vast amount of emotional problems, expressed either psychically or somatically, which affected the bulk of patients I saw. At that time there was almost no psychotherapy available in the National Health Service outside of the few specialized centres in London and the only help to be obtained from the local psychiatric outpatients' department seemed to be the suggestion that patients be given barbiturates to sedate them, or, if that did not help, amphetamines to stimulate them. At about this time, in 1952, I read in the *British Medical Journal* of the successful treatment of a case of congenital ichthyosis, a rare skin disease, in an adolescent boy, by A.A. Mason (now a psychoanalyst) using hypnotic suggestion, and this suggested to me a way in which I might be able to help patients. Following a course of instruction in the technique by him, I started to

7

use it in my practice and in this lay the seeds of my psychoanalytic career.

At first I used hypnotic techniques for the purpose of direct suggestion, but later I used it more for the attempt to recover repressed memories of traumatic experiences with the emotions attached to them, as first described by Breuer and Freud in *Studies in Hysteria* (1895). In a number of cases where I could pinpoint the trauma, this was very successful, but I soon discovered that either I could not reach such experiences or that patients had not had such experiences. Patients would talk in the trance states if requested but I had little appreciation of what they were trying to convey to me by doing so, with the inevitable result that no therapeutic help occurred. I then read books on hypnoanalysis, which recommended that the hypnotherapist have personal therapy in order to help him understand. Interestingly enough, it was psychotherapy and not hypnotherapy that was recommended for the hypnotherapist. I followed up this suggestion, but gradually I gave up using hypnotic techniques and hypnoanalysis as I became progressively psychoanalytically orientated, yet it was my clinical experiences in this intervening period that helped me formulate new concepts of the psychodynamics of the hypnotic state and its phenomena (1963, 1966, 1969).

Before proceeding with these clinical experiences and my own theoretical concepts, I would like first to give a brief account of the main psychoanalytical theorizing on the hypnotic state and relationship from Freud onwards. Freud's first statement on hypnosis was contained in a footnote in his book, *Three Essays on the Theory of Sexuality* (1905), where he stated that the credulous submissiveness of the hypnotized subject 'lies in an unconscious fixation of the subject's libido to the figure of the hypnotist, through the medium of the masochistic components of the sexual instinct'.

Ferenczi, in his essay on 'Introjection and transference' (1909), suggested that the hypnotic state is an expression of the early child–parent relationship, with the subject being the small child and the hypnotist being unconsciously regarded as either its mother or father. He differentiated between the 'maternal' form of hypnosis, where the means of induction into the trance state are gentle and persuasive, and the 'paternal' form, where the means of induction are forceful and authoritarian, such as the eye-stare technique. He thought that the maternal form was based on love and the paternal on fear.

Freud's later contribution to theory was in his book, *Group Psychology and the Analysis of the Ego* (1921). He compared hypnosis with the state of being in love, but with the important difference of there being no sexual satisfaction. He described the hypnotic relationship as a group of two people and suggested that in the unconscious, the hypnotist is put in the place of the subject's ego–ideal. However, he felt that his explanation was insufficient to account for all the observed phenomena.

Ernest Jones, in a paper on 'The nature of autosuggestion' (1923), proposed that the hypnotized subject projected his superego onto the hypnotist. In this way the hypnotist has to fit in with the demands of the subject's conscience and morality – that is his superego, to a fair extent – and if his suggestions offend too much against them, the subject will not obey them.

Paul Schilder (1922) added to these the concept of a masochistic identification of the subject with the hypnotist. The subject, by submitting and abasing himself to the hypnotist in a masochistic manner, identifies himself with the supposed power and authority of the hypnotist which he himself has projected onto the hypnotist.

So far, all the theories have been based on erotic submissiveness and identification, but, with the establishment of the structural theory of the psyche by Freud in *The Ego and the Id* (1923), more attention began to be paid to what is now called ego psychology with the various concepts of the development of the ego and its functioning. L. Kubie and S. Margolin (1944) suggested that hypnosis did not necessarily involve any hypnotic relationship between two people, as a trance-state could be induced by entirely physical means producing sensori-motor deprivation. This meant that the hypnotic state could be entirely accounted for in terms of a regression of ego–functioning, with the subject gradually failing to distinguish between himself and the outside world and so regressing to a primitive infantile state.

This concept was contested by M. Gill and M. Brenman in their book, *Hypnosis and Related States* (1959), in which they maintained that the hypnotic relationship, even if physical manipulations were used for the induction of the trance, was an essential component of that induction. They also agreed that the regression of ego–functions to more primitive modes of behaviour certainly occurred. Thus, the two mechanisms seem necessary – the sensori–motor reduction for the subject and the psychodynamics of the relationship between subject and hypnotist.

Prior to this, Brenman and Gill together with R. Knight (1952) had written on the topic of the subject's hostility towards the hypnotist. They studied fluctuations in the depth of hypnosis of patients in hypnoanalytic treatment and observed changes in depth if the material produced by the patient suggested hostility to the hypnotist. They put forward the hypothesis 'that the hypnotic state involves not only the gratification of pregenital and Oedipal needs but also a constantly changing balance between such needs, experiences of hostility, and defences against both these sets of instinctual impulses'. They further emphasized the more subservient role of the hypnotist in this respect, and it is on these aspects of the hypnotic state that my own theorizing has been elaborated, although at the time when I had been making my own observations and speculating on them, I had not known of this prior work of these authors.

I, too, had found that when I asked patients in the trance-state to free-associate, I noticed that if I interpreted their associations in terms of their hostility to me, the hypnotist, the depth of the trance would considerably lighten. If I persisted in continuing for some time to interpret the negative transference, the patients eventually could no longer be induced into a trance-state at all. I noticed that this phenomenon did not occur if my interpretations were of the positive transference. The conclusion I drew from this was that the hypnotic state could exist only as long as the hostile feelings of the subject towards the hypnotist were not made explicit.

A second observation, a subjective one, has not previously been described in the literature as far as I am aware. Usually I had the feeling as work progressed that I was in control of the patient within this relationship and this made me feel both powerful and elated. However, there were also times that I had the very strong feeling aroused in me that the patient was in control of me and that I was being swept along as a helpless observer by the patient. The only other times I have since had these intense feelings of being so helpless have occurred in the analysis of a chronic schizophrenic patient; for example, he described feeling as though he were a fly being swept along on a giant's foot, and at that moment, that was just the way I was feeling. I am sure that I would not have become aware of these counter-transference feelings of helplessness with my hypnotized patients if I had not been in analysis to help me to become aware of the whole range of my own feelings in my own therapy.

This reference to counter-transference takes me to a brief aside. In 1962 when I presented these views on hypnosis to a Scientific Meeting of the British Psycho-Analytical Society, there was a different atmosphere from the present one on the topic of counter-transference. Although Paula Heimann had published her paper on the subject in 1950, which presented counter-transference as an unconscious communication and not solely as an unanalysed resistance in the analyst, this had not yet been assimilated by the Society. The result was that my courage deserted me in presenting my counter-transference feelings as part of my findings and led to their omission in my original paper on hypnosis, something I now rather regret.

The third element for my speculations is the fact that although the hypnotized subject feels and says that he is under the control of the hypnotist and has little or no volition of his own – that is, that he feels that the hypnotist and not himself is the prime mover in the production of these phenomena – it must be, as Ferenczi (1909) pointed out, that unless one believes in magic, the hypnotic phenomena are primarily the product of the subject's psyche and not of the hypnotist's. This raises an interesting issue; that if the hypnotist were to tell the subject that hypnosis results from the subject's belief in magic and in the supposed omnipotent qualities of the hypnotist, would the subject then go into a hypnotic trance-state? The answer is supplied by L. Wolberg, when he writes:

> During the early phases of hypno-analysis it is unwise to try to alter the patient's fantasies of the magic that he expects from the hypnotic process. To do so will cause him to respond with resistance and will block the emergence of other transference reactions. What he seems to want unconsciously from the relationship is to be able to depend upon a kind and omnipotent person. To inject interpretations at this stage may create panic or such contempt for the analyst as to interfere with achieving the proper trance depth and with the interpersonal relationship itself.
>
> (Wolberg 1945: 240)

To account for these three observations, I am proposing the hypothesis that the hypnotic state is based on a collusive deception between the subject and the hypnotist, a deception based on an unspoken secret agreement that the hypnotist must pretend to the subject that he is omnipotent, all-powerful. Only in this way will the subject go into the trance-state and remain in it. What, then, is the meaning of this secret deception to the unconscious of the subject, which is 'aware' of the pretence? The answer I suggest is that, with the hypnotist's collusion, the subject feels that he is omnipotently forcing the hypnotist to this deception by projecting his own superego and feelings of omnipotence into the hypnotist and is thereby in control of this situation. The hypnotist meanwhile passively accepts these projections (projective identifications) and glories in them in a manic fashion, by his feelings of magical omnipotence in his prowess as a hypnotist. It is only with analytic self-awareness that the hypnotist comes to recognize his feelings of being controlled by the subject and that he has been projecting his own helpless and controlled feelings into the subject. In this dynamic, far from the hypnotic relationship being only a passive, masochistic identification and surrender on the part of the subject, the unconscious content also includes these

11

omnipotent, controlling, hostile aspects of the subject which are being acted out. The hypnotic state can be conceived as a collusion between hypnotist and subject to deny this hostile attack, and, at the same time, it is an expression of this attack. This formulation makes this state comparable to a hysterical symptom with the repression or denial of the impulse and its expression in another form, but, in this instance, with the necessary condition of the hypnotist's collusion. This aspect makes it resemble a *folie-à-deux*.

This hypothesis of the more active unconscious controlling mechanisms working in the subject's psyche would account for the fact that the hypnotized subject cannot be made to produce phenomena that he resists. The situation resembles that in the fable of the frog and the ox whereby the 'frog'-hypnotist is being omnipotently transformed by the subject into the 'puffed-up ox' hypnotist. An analogy of the situation as that of one aspect of the British Constitution. Here there is a monarch who has all the trappings of power, with a parliament that swears allegiance and subservience to the monarchy, whereas the true situation is, of course, that the power is really in the hands of the subservient parliament with the all-powerful monarch being unable to do anything without its consent.

If this hypothesis is correct, there should be evidence of anxieties in the patient about the outcome of this hostile attack on the hypnotist, and these anxieties would be either of a persecutory type from fear of retaliation by the hypnotist, or of a depressive type from fear of the guilt engendered by the attack. It is a commonly observed fact that occasionally there are spontaneous outbursts of anxiety in the hypnotized subject for no apparent reason and these can be manifestations of either type of anxiety. It can also help to explain other observable phenomena encountered in the trance-state, such as the subject's capacity for considerably heightened performance, in the subject's ability for reality testing at the hypnotist's suggestion, and the subject's ability to produce various forms of hallucinatory phenomena, which deny reality testing, such as visual hallucinations, anaesthesias, aphonia, and so on. It is clear that the subject fits in very strongly with the hypnotist's suggestions in an almost compulsive fashion in order to avoid the anxieties that would otherwise be aroused. It is noticeable that if the subject does not comply with the hypnotist's suggestions, intense anxiety is aroused in the subject, a situation akin to the anxiety aroused in an obsessional patient if he does not carry out his obsessional rituals. Since these obsessional activities are regarded as being of a reparative nature, to undo the damage caused by the patient's unconscious hostility, this lends support to the notion of the hypnotized subject's compliance being of the same order. In this way the guilt of the subject will be a powerful factor in reinforcing the hypnotic state.

This dynamic would also help to explain observations made by Wolberg which arose when he did interpret the subject's hostility to the hypnoanalyst but at a much later stage of the therapy. He wrote:

The question may be asked whether an analysis of the hypnotic interpersonal relationship may not remove the very motivations that make hypnosis possible. In the vast majority of cases it has no such effect; usually a peculiar dissociation exists. The patient continues to react to hypnosis, going into trance-states while at the same time manifesting hostile feelings towards the analyst. Rarely does resistance developing out of analysis of the transference become so intense that the patient refuses to enter hypnosis.

(Wolberg 1945)

I would suggest that the 'peculiar dissociation' that he describes implies a split in the ego, and that this split has occurred because the accumulation of guilt in the patient towards the hypnotist has reached such an intensity that the hostility can be explored only by means of such a split. This will mean that this split-off area cannot be explored in the course of a hypnoanalysis, which means it is doomed from the start to be incomplete.

A further observation frequently observed is that when a subject emerges from the trance-state, he tends to use certain types of phrase such as 'I feel marvellous', 'Never felt better in my life', and the tone of a rather manic euphoria in these statements is unmistakable. This manic state may well reflect feelings of triumph experienced by the subject following on the successful attack on the hypnotist. Furthermore, the occasional headache, paraesthesia, and so forth, which may be complained of, may well represent a somatizing of a depressive state, resulting from the guilt for the attack.

To summarize, the hypnotic state represents a collusive manic denial of an omnipotent, controlling, hostile attack on the hypnotist, together with the denial of anxieties of retaliation and guilt associated with it. This is a form of the manic defence, albeit in a two-person situation, exhibiting the other characteristics of this defence: splitting, projective identification, denial, omnipotence, idealization, and ambivalence.

A patient of mine on emerging from the trance-state was asked to tell me about his feelings in the trance. He said, 'I thought you went deeper in hypnosis – that you were in control of the hypnotist.' This unconscious omission – he meant to say 'in the control of the hypnotist' – illustrates the thesis presented here. It was these insights that helped me to relinquish hypnoanalysis for psychoanalysis, since I could not accept participating in a collusive experience which by its very nature could not be examined and analysed.

Two of the phenomena that could be observed in the hypnotic state and particularly interested me were those of consciousness and of negative hallucinations, and I want to examine them more closely from a psychoanalytical viewpoint. Let me first quote from Freud's case history of Miss Lucy R. in his 'Studies on hysteria' (Breuer and Freud 1895) where he is recapitulating his observations of Hippolyte Bernheim at work with hypnotized patients:

> I was saved from this new embarrassment by remembering that I had myself seen Bernheim producing evidence that the memories of events during somnambulism are only apparently forgotten in the waking state and can be revived by a mild word of command and a pressure with the hand intended to give a different state of consciousness. He had, for instance, given a woman in a state of somnambulism a negative hallucination to the effect that he was no longer present, and had then endeavoured to draw attention to himself in a great variety of ways, including some of a decidedly aggressive kind. He did not succeed. After she had woken up he asked her to tell him what he had done to her while she thought he was not there. She replied in surprise that she knew nothing of it. But he did not accept this. He insisted that she could remember everything and laid his hand on her forehead to help her to recall it. And lo and behold! she ended by describing everything that she had ostensibly not perceived during her somnambulism and ostensibly not remembered in her waking state.
>
> (Breuer and Freud 1895: 109)

If we examine this accurate and concise account, it can be agreed that the subject was not in a state of consciousness in the ordinary sense of the word. There had been an obvious interruption in the continuity of her normal conscious experience while in the trance, since she did not easily remember events occurring during this period. Her entire attention had been focused on the hypnotist, so that no one would have been able to establish rapport with the subject unless the hypnotist had suggested such a rapport to the subject. Furthermore, sensory perception by the subject showed little evidence of having any psychic quality – to use a term of Freud's – unless the subject is commanded to do so by the hypnotist. If the hypnotist were simply to hypnotize and then leave the subject, the subject would remain inert, would be incapable of being aroused by another person, and would only return to a normal conscious state after falling into a deep sleep. This suggests that the perception of psychic quality, which is the suggested hallmark of the sense organ called consciousness, the system Cs, is absent during the trance-state, except at the hypnotist's command.

What did Freud mean by the term 'psychic quality'? It was first used by him in the document, 'Project for a scientific psychology' (1895), which was his attempt to explain mental functioning in neurological terms. Although he soon abandoned neurological explanations, the document in fact contained within itself the nucleus of many of his later psychological theories. To quote from the 'Project':

> Consciousness gives us what are called qualities – sensations which are different in a great multiplicity of ways and whose difference is distinguished according to its relations with the external world. Within this difference there are series, similarities and so on.
>
> (Freud 1895: 308)

In the famous Chapter 7 of *The Interpretation of Dreams* (1900) on the psychology of the dream-processes, where he 'translated' some of his neurological concepts into psychology, he defined consciousness as the sense-organ for the perceptions of psychical qualities; thought-processes acquire quality by becoming associated with verbal memories, with language, and so attract the attention of consciousness. In this context, quality would seem to equate with meaning and significance.

In the hypnotic state, it seems that the system, consciousness, is absent and that the psychical qualities that the subject responds to are those suggested by the hypnotist. One could hypothesize that the sense-organ, consciousness, has been projected onto the hypnotist and that the subject must compulsively follow the hypnotist's verbal commands in place of his own perceptions, which are denied. We recognize this denial since they can be recovered to consciousness on emerging from the trance-state as in Freud's description.

W. Bion (1957) suggested the concept of a bizarre object to account for certain phenomena of schizophrenic patients. Briefly, he suggested that parts of the ego – the perceptual apparatus – could be subjected to sadistic splitting attacks and projected to penetrate or encyst objects, giving rise to a bizarre object. He thought that 'the object, angered at being engulfed, swells up, so to speak, and suffuses and controls the piece of personality that engulfs it' (1957: 267). Hypnosis is not a severe psychotic illness or manifestation but, if in this state, the subject splits his perceptual apparatus, his consciousness, and projects it into the hypnotist, the hypnotist could now function as a bizarre consciousness for the subject, even to the extent of the hypnotist engaging, and revelling, in swelling up, suffusing and controlling activities as I have earlier described.

If we now turn to negative hallucination, it would be helpful to consider an actual experimental situation in order to examine the phenomenon in detail. The setting is that of the hypnotist, his hypnotized subject, and a third person, P., sitting in a chair. The hypnotist suggests to the subject that P. is no longer in the room and that he should describe the chair as he sees it. The subject will then proceed to describe the chair including those parts of the chair that will be hidden from his view by P., who is still sitting in the chair. The description of these hidden aspects are, of course, imaginative on the subject's part. The subject is then told to sit in the chair and he will attempt to do so but is obviously prevented from this as P. is already sitting there. The hypnotist then asks him why he cannot sit in the chair and the subject will attempt some explanation for his inability to do so – but never offers the correct explanation that someone is already sitting there. The subject is then pressed by the hypnotist that the explanation given is obviously faulty and that a better one be found. The subject will now either become extremely agitated and emerge from the trance or perhaps withdraw into a deep sleep. In either case, the hypnotic state has been brought to an end by this pressure from the hypnotist.

We can now consider the problem of the constitution of a negative hallucination. From Freud's quotation on page 14, we know that the subject does 'observe' everything that has taken place during the trance-state and this must constitute one level of mental registration. We also know that the subject is not 'seeing' the person in the chair, and this means that there must be a denial or disavowal of these sensory perceptions, and this constitutes a second level of registration. Thirdly, we know that the subject does not describe a blank or a space when asked to describe what he sees, but instead fills the blank space with a description of what he thinks should be there, a sort of positive hallucination, which is a third registration. So it would appear that the sensory-perceptual ego splits into three parts – one that registers the sensory perception, one that denies it, and one that hallucinatorally fills in the denial on a rationalizing basis. So long as no attempt is made to question this rationalization, the arrangement is a stable one, but as soon as it is questioned, as was done after the subject was asked to sit in the 'empty' chair, the situation became fraught with intense anxieties.

The question now arises as to the possible causes of this phenomenon and I would suggest the following as possible answers to the question. First, for the subject to acknowledge that he cannot sit in the chair as someone is already there, he must also acknowledge that he is not seeing the person because the hypnotist has given him such a

16

suggestion. In all hypnotic phenomena, the subject will never say that he is acting in such-and-such a way because the hypnotist has told him to, and I believe that the reason for this is the essential ambivalent, collusive nature of the hypnotic state. To acknowledge the hypnotist as the source of the suggestion would be to release the very anxieties that are being denied in this state, and this is demonstrated by the severe anxiety experienced from the hypnotist's pressure to do so.

Second, there is some sort of equilibrium in the ego-functioning when it is split into the three parts to produce the negative hallucination. However, when the hypnotist attempts to produce the situation whereby the denial of the visual perception of the person P. is being tested by sensory perceptions from other sense-organs – that is, those of touch and pressure on the subject's body when he attempts to sit in the chair already containing P. – the subject is faced with the task of attempting to reconcile and integrate these differing and contradictory sensory impressions. This can only be made compatible with the maintenance of the hypnotic state by even further ego-splitting, with the result that this excessive splitting becomes too great a threat to the synthetic integrating functioning of the ego, with the production of a psychotic state. It is from this also that the subject recoils in acute anxiety. To put it another way, the already split ego has to introject a contradictory split hypnotist – an impossible task.

To conclude, I want to take up the question as to why the subject needs the positive hallucinatory level of rationalization as one of the features of this phenomenon. I believe that to 'see' a blank space, a 'nothing-space', is to see the negative of the object, a no-thing, and this negation is halfway towards acknowledging the presence of the denied object. In this way, the subject is not fully carrying out the hypnotist's suggestion and this in itself will arouse intense anxieties for all of the reasons already discussed.

Note

1 First version published in the *International Journal of Psycho-Analysis*, 1963, 44: 372–4 and the *International Journal of Psycho-Analysis*, 1966, 47: 50–3.

2

Jocasta: crimes and collusion[1]

When still a student at the Institute of Psycho-Analysis, I went to a Scientific Meeting of the British Society on a topic that I do not now remember. During the ensuing discussion, Paula Heimann made the comment that Oedipus did not die whereas Jocasta did, and this remark stuck in my mind. It stimulated many thoughts and eventually resulted in a paper on the subject of Jocasta's crimes (1961). As far as I am aware, this was the first psychoanalytical paper to focus on the role of Jocasta in the Oedipus story and of her relationship with him.

Since the earliest days of psychoanalysis when Freud first used the Oedipus myth to illustrate his clinical findings, the themes of the story have been taken up by several writers. The earlier writers devoted their attention to Oedipus, but more recently the other protagonists in the triangle have been brought into the limelight. George Devereux (1953) examined the role of Laius, Jocasta's husband and Oedipus' father, and linked it with his homosexuality, which, though not described or touched on in the play, *Oedipus Rex*, by Sophocles, was manifest in accounts of the Greek myth. Mark Kanzer (1950), in his analysis of the Oedipus trilogy of plays by Sophocles, saw Jocasta as a potential pre-Oedipal 'bad mother' in the eyes of her son. This concept of the mother being an object of her son's hostility was further developed by H. van der Sterren (1952). To quote from his paper:

It may be interesting to enquire what motives are given in Sophocles' drama for the son's hostility towards his mother. In the first place there is the sadistic element of the sexual passion; then there is the fact that Jocasta and Merope forbid him to think about his origin, and therein we find the fact that the mother does not allow her little son to satisfy his Oedipal desires. Indeed she helps father to restrict and punish her son, and sends him away from her presence. . . . Finally it is clear that Oedipus is hostile towards his mother and that he even desires her death because her seductive powers bring him into danger of punishment and guilty conscience.

(van der Sterren 1952: 343)

The story of Oedipus is sufficiently well known not to need repetition here, and the text I am using for the examination of my theme is Sophocles' play *Oedipus Rex* in its translation by E.F. Watling in the Penguin Classics series. There are two puzzling features in the text that, so far, seem to have been neither noticed nor explained. The first relates to the actual punishments of both Oedipus and Jocasta, the remark that first sparked my interest. Oedipus has apparently been responsible for committing the two crimes of incest and parricide, yet his punishment consisted only of self-blinding and banishment from Thebes, and even this was delayed for many years. Jocasta has apparently committed only the crime of incest, yet her punishment is suicide. Why this disparity and why is the punishment of Jocasta so much more severe than that of Oedipus?

The second feature is equally puzzling. It has always been assumed that Oedipus has been guilty of committing both incest and parricide, yet on a careful reading of the play, it becomes evident that it is only for the crime of incest that explicit proof is offered. As I shall later show, it is never explicitly decided whose account of the scene at the crossroads is the correct one – that of Oedipus or that of the one-time palace servant, now shepherd. Yet both Oedipus and Jocasta independently assume that Oedipus' version is the correct one – this following the explicit proof of incest. The question here is why proof of incest is apparently proof of parricide for both Oedipus and Jocasta.

In the light of these two enigmas, let us turn to the play and pay particular attention to the activities and statements of Jocasta and consider the following points:

1 On p.45, Jocasta is telling Oedipus of the fate of the child born to her and Laius, and says:

> As for the child
> It was not yet three days old, when he cast it out
> (By other hands, not his) with riveted ankles
> To perish on the empty mountain-side.

Later, on p.58, Oedipus learns that the 'other hands' were those of Jocasta.

> Oedipus: She gave it you?
> Shepherd: Yes, master.

19

What was the reason for Jocasta's wanting to hide this fact from Oedipus?

2 On p.46, Jocasta tells Oedipus of the servant who had returned from the scene at the crossroads:

> When he came back
> And found you king in his late master's place,
> He earnestly begged me to let him go away
> Into the country to become a shepherd,
> Far from the city's eyes. I let him go.
> Poor fellow, he might have asked a greater favour.

We may ask the questions, why he did not wish to serve under the new king, and why he might have asked a 'greater favour'. This implies that he has performed some special service for Jocasta to merit this.

3 On p.47, Oedipus relates to Jocasta the story of his boyhood and the incident in which his descent from Polybus and Merope, the rulers of Corinth, was called into question. This had led him to consult the Pythian oracle for the truth about his parents, and he received the unexpected answer:

> . . . how I must marry my mother,
> And become the parent of a misbegotten brood,
> An offence to all mankind – and kill my father.

The implication of this is that the greater offence to mankind is incest, not parricide. What is the reason for this paradox?

4 On p.46, Jocasta describes to Oedipus the constitution of the Theban party at the crossroads:

> Five men in all, a herald leading them;
> One carriage only, in which King Laius rode.
> *Oedipus*: Clearer, alas too clear! Who told you this?
> *Jocasta*: A servant, the only survivor that returned.

Later, on p.48, Oedipus describes his experiences at the crossroads:

> . . . I met
> A herald followed by a horse-drawn carriage, and a man
> Seated therein, just as you have described.
> The leader roughly ordered me out of the way;
> And his venerable master joined in with a surly command.
> It was the driver that thrust me aside, at him I struck
> For I was angry. The old man saw it, leaning from the carriage,
> Waiting, until I passed, then, seizing for a weapon

The driver's two-pronged goad, struck me on the head.
He paid with interest for his temerity;
Quick as lightning, the staff in this right hand
Did its work; he tumbled headlong out of the carriage,
And every man of them there I killed.

In this account, Oedipus describes the party as consisting of four men – the herald, the man in the carriage, the leader, and the driver. If this is so, how do we account for the servant's statement, the only survivor from the crossroads incident, who had reported to Jocasta that there were five men?

5 On p.54, the messenger from Corinth tells his story about being entrusted with a baby on Mount Cithaeron, and says to Oedipus:

The infirmity in your ankles tells the tale.

This implies that there is a very obvious infirmity in the ankles of Oedipus, and if this tells the tale to the messenger, why did it not tell the tale to Jocasta, who knew of the riveted ankles and the curse on Laius?

6 On p.54, Oedipus wishes to know if anyone knows the whereabouts of the shepherd, the ex-servant of Laius, to whom he had been given as a baby. The following then occurs:

Chorus: I think he will prove to be that same countryman
Whom you have already asked to see. The Queen
Is the one most able to tell you if this is so.
Oedipus: My wife. You know the man whom we have sent for.
Is that the man he means?
Jocasta (white with terror): What does it matter
What man he means? It makes no difference now . . .,
Forget what he has told you. . . . It makes no difference.

If the two shepherds to be sent for are really one and the same person and Jocasta is quite aware of this, what is the explanation for her terror in this situation and its absence in the previous situation when he is to be called as a witness of the crossroads scene?

7 On p.55, before her final exit, Jocasta says to Oedipus:

Doomed man! O never live to learn the truth.

Yet Oedipus does live, and to a ripe old age, but does he ever really learn the whole truth?

8 On p.58, Oedipus, on having had explicit proof of his incest says:

Revealed as I am, sinful in my begetting,
Sinful in marriage, sinful in shedding of blood!

Yet it is has not been explicitly proved that he did in fact spill his father's blood. We must also wonder the meaning of the phrase 'sinful in my begetting'.

9 On p.60, Jocasta's attendant who quotes her last words before her suicide, says:

> Remembering the son she bore long since, the son
> By whom the sire was slain, the son to whom
> The mother bore yet other children . . .

Jocasta also assumes the guilt of Oedipus for parricide, and yet she could not have heard Oedipus accuse himself of this crime as she had already left him before he did so. What is the reason for her assumption of this?

At this point, we should pause for a moment. So far, I have been using the text of the play as though the characters in it, created by the dramatist, were actually real people caught up in a dramatic situation with motivations, both conscious and unconscious, of their own. That one is led to feel that this is the case attests to the greatness of the creator, Sophocles, in giving such credible flesh and blood to a myth current at the time in the culture of Athens. What I am actually doing is looking at the creations of Sophocles' mind and seeing how, through his own unconscious processes responding to the themes of the myth, and his dramatic abilities, he could create such a text that allows one to examine it for inconsistencies and conclusions that might help to explain various psychological questions aroused by the myth. This may then throw light on phantasies common to all human psyches and not simply that of Sophocles. From the sparse facts that are known of the life of Sophocles, there is no evidence that such problems of incest or parricide were in reality part of his family experience.

To return to our queries about the text of the play, I want to suggest a possible reconstruction of the story that would explain them, and then to see if there is any other further evidence to support this reconstruction.

To begin the story, we must recapitulate the birth of Oedipus. Laius had abducted the youth Chrysippus before his marriage to Jocasta, and a curse was proclaimed on him by Hera, the Mother-Goddess, as a punishment for his homosexuality. The curse was that if Laius had a son, the child would kill him and marry his wife in his place. Under those circumstances Laius refused Jocasta her marriage right to children, until eventually she raped him when he was drunk and this resulted in the birth of Oedipus. This may be the reason why Oedipus proclaimed himself to be 'sinful in my begetting'. When Oedipus was three days old, Laius decided that he should die from exposure on the mountain and had his ankles riveted, yet he did not carry out the exposure himself. Perhaps his homosexual love was too strong for him, and instead he left it to his wife to carry out his orders. She gave Oedipus to the servant with ostensible instructions to allow the child to die on Mount Cithaeron, but then, not wishing her longed-for son to die, intimated to the servant by gesture, tone of voice or possibly directly in words, that the baby's life should be spared. This would explain the terror described in (6), as at this stage an independent witness to the survival was present, the messenger from Corinth, and the servant-shepherd would have been unable to lie, if really pressed about his saving of Oedipus in response to Jocasta's wishes. In addition to her love for her son, her own complicity in saving Oedipus to enact the curse would then be brought to light, and reveal her hatred of Laius for his frustration of her sexual needs and desires. The emphasis, by both the Chorus and Oedipus, on Jocasta's knowledge of the identity of the servant is another pointer to her complicity.

Oedipus was then brought up in the house of Polybus and Merope at Corinth as though he were their child until he was made doubtful of his parentage, which made him consult the oracle and learned of the curse. Leaving Corinth, he met Laius and his retinue at the crossroads, where presumably the servant was lagging behind. On witnessing the killings, the servant reported the scene to Jocasta on his return to Thebes, presumably describing the killer as a young man with infirm ankles. Whether he reported to her before or after her marriage to Oedipus is of little significance to her complicity. This then would explain the disparity in numbers, four or five men, mentioned in (4). She, realizing that this young man with infirm ankles who had killed her husband was most probably her son, made the servant swear to tell a different story about a band of robbers murdering Laius, and this was, most probably, the special service for which a 'greater favour' would have been justified, mentioned in (2). As well as this, since there were no other witnesses of the scene, she did not fear Oedipus sending for him in his capacity as witness, which is in marked contrast to the terror felt when he was to testify to the exposure scene when an independent witness was present (6).

Oedipus, having killed Laius, now proceeded to defeat the Sphinx by answering her riddle correctly, which made him entitled to become Jocasta's husband. His obvious attention and satisfaction of her sexual needs is manifest by the birth of their four children, Etiocles, Polynices, Ismene and Antigone. It would indeed be strange if Jocasta did not know his identity if this reconstruction is valid. The rest of the story now follows in Oedipus discovering his origins and incest. The truth that he never learns is of Jocasta's complicity in the enactment of the curse.

The proposal being put forward here is that Jocasta was entirely aware of events and had an active complicity in them. There is some other evidence to support this point of view, which was probably known to Sophocles, who was a well-educated Athenian:

1 Devereux quotes Otto Rank for source material that the combat at the crossroads took place in the presence of Jocasta and that incest occurred immediately afterwards. In this version of the myth and in the light of the curse, the identity of the murderer must have been obvious to Jocasta.
2 In the account given by Robert Graves (1955) in his book on Greek myths, he describes an incident that is not mentioned in the play. Teiresias, the blind prophet, revealed to Oedipus that the plague in Thebes, which followed Oedipus' marriage to Jocasta, would cease only if a Sown Man were to die for the sake of the city. In response to this, Jocasta's father, Menoeceus, who was one of those who had risen from the earth when Cadmus had sown the dragon's teeth – that is, he was a Sown Man – leaped from the city walls to his death. This was, however, of no avail in abating the plague – presumably the wrong man had died, but from our point of view, it suggests Jocasta's complicity through her father in causing the plague.
3 On p.33 of the play, Oedipus states that he had sent for Teiresias to unravel the mystery of the plague on the advice of Creon, Jocasta's brother. Once again, Jocasta is linked to the plague.

If these speculations are valid, we can understand why Jocasta dies and Oedipus lives. From the beginning, she has consciously wanted Laius' death. It should be noted that after the murder of Laius, his death was not investigated to apprehend and punish the murderer as the Sphinx was on the scene. Since the Sphinx may be identified with aspects of Jocasta, as we shall see later, one might say that she did not want the murderer punished, since he was her son. Her incest was also a conscious act; hence her crimes of wanting and not punishing her husband's death and of seducing her son in full knowledge are more deserving of punishment than those of Oedipus, who could claim ignorance. This could apply to any similar mother–son relationship; her seduction of the child and destruction of the father's authority, even if the father colludes with this, is carried out in the full light of her own adult authority and responsibility. The son can claim his childhood immaturity as a mitigating factor in the performance of his wishes. This, then, would explain the absence of the talion punishment for Oedipus and its presence for Jocasta concerning the murder of

Laius. It would also explain why she assumes Oedipus is guilty of parricide, for she has known it all along and has wished for it to take place.

So far we have concentrated on Jocasta and her complicity, but we should now turn to Oedipus. Are there any indications of complicity from his side? I would suggest the following:

1 On p.45, Jocasta has told Oedipus of the exposure of her infant, apparently for the first time in their relationship. However, this event was not considered a secret so it would have been common knowledge in the palace. Under these circumstances, it would have been extraordinary if Oedipus had not known of it, too, after marrying Jocasta.

2 Assuming that Oedipus had known of the exposure, how is it that Oedipus had never made any link, however speculative, between the exposure and the ankle-riveting, and his own infirm ankles?

3 On p.47, Oedipus speaks of being told in Corinth that he was not the son of Polybus. Even though both Polybus and Merope deny this strongly, Oedipus remained unconvinced and so went to the oracle. Why did he remain unconvinced, and why had he never wondered why his ankles had been riveted?

The implication of these suggestions is that there were many secrets in the family at Corinth, and presumably at Thebes, that were to be neither spoken of openly, nor speculated upon too freely. In this way, Oedipus maintains a more unconscious complicity in the events, similar to a state of denial or negation. As in the discussion on hypnosis in the previous chapter, a collusive relationship exists between Oedipus and Jocasta, not to know or understand too much, to maintain the family secrets, and above all, to deny the existence of hostility, murderous feelings and guilt that are present in the relationship. In this instance, the destructiveness and guilt are related to a three-person relationship rather than a two-person one as in the hypnosis relationship. The son may collude with his mother in remaining barely aware of secrets that she is keeping from him, in the interests of what he believes are to his advantage. She can in this way be made the repository for his projected destructive and hostile wishes towards his father and incestuous ones towards her.

The self-blinding of Oedipus is usually regarded as his punishment for incest and parricide, but there is another aspect of this concerning talion punishment that is of interest. The talion is usually regarded as involving the identity of punishment for the crime with the crime itself; an eye for an eye and a tooth for a tooth. There is another less-known talion. If a person accuses another of committing a crime and then fails to prove his case, a punishment is exacted on the accuser which is identical with that which the accused would have suffered had he been proved guilty. On p.35 of the play, Oedipus is asking Teiresias, the blind seer, to tell what he knows of the murderer of Laius, and he refuses. Oedipus becomes angry and accuses Teiresias of plotting the murder and even of doing it himself if he had not been blind. This accusation involves the blindness of Teiresias, so perhaps part of Oedipus' self-blinding is the talion punishment for not proving his accusation.

In Graves's account of the blinding of Teiresias, he gives three different versions and all involve sexual knowledge. Perhaps the third version is most relevant here. The story is of Teiresias adjudicating at a beauty contest between Aphrodite and the Three Graces and awarding the prize to Cale, one of the Graces, whereupon Aphrodite turned him into an old woman. Some days later, Hera, the Mother-Goddess, was reproaching Zeus for his infidelities, but he argued that when he did share her couch, she had the most enjoyable time by far. 'Women, of course, derive infinitely greater pleasure from the sexual act than men.' 'What nonsense!' cried Hera, 'The exact contrary is the case, and well you know it!' Teiresias, summoned to settle the dispute from his personal experiences, answered:

If the parts of love-pleasure be counted as ten,
Thrice three go to women, one only to men.

Hera was so exasperated by Zeus's triumphant smile that she blinded Teiresias, whereupon Zeus compensated him with inward sight and a life extended to seven generations. Possibly blindness was the punishment for Oedipus too on perceiving the intensity of his mother's sexual desires and particularly towards her own son.

Can this constellation of a woman who has murderous wishes towards her husband and incestuous ones towards her son be substantiated in any other field of scientific investigation apart from psychoanalysis? The answer comes from anthropology. In 1933, Lord Raglan, the English anthropologist, wrote a study called *Jocasta's Crime*, the crime being incest. He described a marked degree of uniformity among primitive creation myths and rituals no matter from what part of the world or in which particular culture they arose, and that the uniform common feature was that they were all incestuous in nature. He reduced the myths to a basic pattern: the world is overwhelmed by a flood and the inhabitants are drowned; the gods kill a giant and from him make a new world; the gods create a human brother and sister and place them in the world; at the instigation of the sister, they mate and become the ancestors of a new race of humans. He suggested that a creation rite was enacted in primitive societies to symbolize this myth and briefly, in the ritual, there is a king-brother and queen-sister; every year the king is killed and his heart eaten by the queen; the queen then has a new mate for the following year, after which he too is killed and a new mate taken. Thus the king is being mated with by the queen and then killed and the cycle repeated. The emphasis is on the activity and instigation of the queen.

The resemblances between these myths and rites and the incest and parricide of the Oedipus story as outlined here are very close. Raglan made another point about incest in that there were two conflicting attitudes towards it in primitive societies. One attitude was that it was taboo and punishable by death; he had his own reasons for this and they were not Freud's. The other attitude is that incest secures survival after death for a man. In Ancient Egypt and Persia, marriage with one's sister, or mother after father had died, was the most highly regarded and sacred union. Now it is well known that in Egypt the fact of death was intensely denied, with the rituals of embalming and preserving the dead and putting the bodies in large tombs together with servants, animals, food, clothes, and so on. I then wondered whether something similar occurred in the burial practices of Ancient Persia to deny death in this way, and was delighted to discover in the *Encyclopaedia of Religion and Ethics* (1927), under 'Burial customs', that in fact this was so. I would postulate that if the death of the father, or brother in his place, can be denied so extremely, then incest can now be allowed and sanctified by society; there is a complete denial of parricidal guilt and its transformation into its manic opposite, sanctification.

Robert Graves has suggested that the Oedipus story represents the change-over from a matrilineal society of the type described above, to the patrilineal, where the line of descent runs through the males. If this is correct, then behind the picture of the powerful male line of Laius and Oedipus is the old matrilineal figure Jocasta, and her eclipse is all the more moving for this not being made obvious in the play. This, together with her complicity in the tragedy as suggested here, would also help explain its very moving quality from another aspect. If all were as obvious as it seems, the story would almost represent a clinical case history in which all motivation becomes clear, and this would have the effect of removing much of the tension. That this does not happen suggests that something must be hidden, and this well relates to Jocasta's hidden role.

The anthropologist Sir James Frazer, in his influential work *The Golden Bough* (1932), remarked: 'No doubt, the poet and his hearers set down these public calamities in great part to the guilt of parricide, which rested on Oedipus; but they can hardly have failed to lay much also of the evil at the door of his incest with his mother.' In primitive societies, incest was believed to be followed by blight and failure of the crops, and the punishment required to expiate the blight was to kill the incestuous pair. However, it is also the case that many fertility rites to encourage the growth of crops are symbolically incestuous. This reminds us of children's games where what would be punishable if actually performed became the precise opposite if performed symbolically. Can one in fact divorce incest from parricide? Can the son possess the mother without first destroying the father? And can the mother have an incestuous relationship with her son without first killing her husband? This may well be the reason for the assumption that if the crime of incest is proved, this implies the proof of killing of the husband-father.

This is a general problem for women as much as for men. For example, many women, out of penis envy, wish to deny and denigrate the role of the man's penis and to control it for themselves. From these wishes arise the wish for parthenogenesis, to be able to procreate without the necessity of the man's penis. Incest with her son may come nearest to putting this phantasy into practice, since if the son is regarded and treated as part of his mother, his penis is her penis and mother and son are a phantasy unity. The husband's penis, after the conception of the son, can then be denied and destroyed. This was an especial problem for Jocasta, who was almost completely denied Laius' penis because of his homosexuality. One might wonder, although there is no evidence to support it, whether her marrying such a man was related to an incestuous relationship with her father, Menoeceus, who did, after all, commit suicide to try to expiate the blight on Thebes.

We have so far been speculating on Jocasta's role in the play but now a further problem arises: what else was motivating her in addition to the suggestions I have just mentioned? I would suggest that a clue is contained in the mode of her suicide, which was by hanging. The Sphinx has another name, which is the 'throttler', since she killed her victims by this means, and clearly hanging oneself is a form of throttling. This would imply that the Sphinx symbolically has throttled Jocasta, and I would suggest that the Sphinx, the terrifying phallic woman, is the embodiment of the projected internal, persecutory, murderous mother-figure of Jocasta's superego. This internal object has been constantly denied, split-off and projected by Jocasta, and in this way, she had positively enjoyed her incestuous relationship with Oedipus and denied the guilt for Laius' murder. It was only when the incest was revealed that the denial could no longer be maintained and the split-off persecutory figure returned with the consequence of the guilt-ridden throttling.

In the differing versions of the myths, there is no available reference to Jocasta's mother or her relationship with her. One might speculate that if her mother was persecutory, she needed to assuage her by being a bad mother and might have used her child for this purpose, first by abandoning him as an infant, then by using him to kill her husband, and then by using him for mating purposes. We might extend these speculations to Oedipus and wonder if he needed to assuage a persecutory mother by being a bad son, first as an infant by turning from the bad Jocasta to the good Merope, then by killing his father, and finally by using his mother for mating. In this way the methods used by both mother and son to deal with persecutory mothers are mutually complementary.

In summary, I have presented a previously hidden picture of Jocasta who has responsibility for two crimes, the murder of her husband and incest with her son, both in full awareness, and that these crimes were committed as a means of dealing with an internal, persecutory, murderous maternal, superego figure. She and Oedipus have had a collusive relationship to deny knowledge of their complicity in these crimes, which only marginally collapses when the true evidence eventually emerges into the open.

Note

1 First version published in the *International Journal of Psycho-Analysis*, 1961, 42: 424–30.

3

Changes in the experiencing of the dream and transference[1]

I first became interested in the experiencing of the dream from observations on a female patient that I made during the course of her analysis with me. The aspect that I want to discuss concerns the dreamer's experience of herself in relationship to the events in the dream and the changes of this experience that can occur during the course of the analysis. I am concerned with this one aspect of the manifest content of the dream as reported by the dreamer and its relationship to the state of transference at the time of the dream. This experiential aspect of the dream should not be confused with the various emotions that the dreamer might feel during the course of a dream. A fairly healthy person might experience her dreams as though she were actively involved in the varying events in the dream, or else as though she were passively observing them from a distance, or perhaps alternating between activity or passivity, but she would not feel that only one sort of experience was, as it were, allowed to her in her dreams to the exclusion of all others. She might experience varying emotions during the course of the dream such as fear, anger, or jealousy, but these are not the same sort of experiences as the former and it is with them that I am concerned.

The patient, whose analysis lasted about six years, was a young woman who had been a voluntary patient in a mental hospital for three years. She was suffering from a borderline schizophrenic psychosis with a severe and crippling urinary disturbance. She was confused about her body image in that she could not be sure where her physical boundaries were, since they were constantly changing, rather like Alice in Wonderland; she was confused about the identity of the person she happened to be with and found it difficult to distinguish herself from that person; didn't know whether she had actually been speaking or only thinking; didn't know whether her dreams were dreams or actual reality; was almost sure there were people inside her who came out to play with her when she was alone; was almost sure that God had appeared to her and spoken with her, and that her younger brother was really her son whom God had given her via her mother's body. She was depersonalized, experienced derealization, did not know whether she was ill or not, but then could not understand why she could not think and that everything seemed so strange. A devilish mother-figure who lived in a far-off provincial town persecuted her, and she worshipped a benign father-God up in the heavens.

During the first two years of the analysis, the transference relationship was characterized by my being experienced as something potentially helpful or harmful, probably unnecessary, rather unreal and at a great distance from her or else confused with her. I was usually felt to be watching or spying on her. There was little sense of involvement with me in the analysis. She was, however, a prolific dreamer of long, detailed, and involved dreams, and it was the working with and interpreting of her dreams that played an important part in the progress of the analysis. As I previously mentioned, she was not quite sure whether she had dreamed her dreams or whether she had actually lived them in reality. It is a common observation that psychotic and non-psychotic patients experience their dreams as concrete reality and this can be conceptualized on the basis of the process of symbolization. Hanna Segal (1957) put forward the concept that psychotics use symbols as substitutes for instinctual activities, whereas neurotics and healthy persons use them, not as substitutes, but as representatives of these activities. Since an essential process in dream formation is the dream-work involving symbolization, this difference in the use of symbols will become manifest in the experience of the dream content. My patient was on the border between substitution and representation and because of this experienced great difficulty in distinguishing between them. One experience of herself in her dreams was that it was a piece of reality; yet at the same time she also experienced it as a dream, and it is to this aspect that I shall now turn.

In her dreams she felt that it was like being in a cinema or theatre watching activities that were proceeding on the screen or stage, but she never felt any sense of herself participating in these activities, even though in some of them that she was watching, she herself was one of the protagonists. Her experience was that of the passive onlooker or watcher and rarely that of the active participant. Events were experienced as being at a distance. This mirrored both her relationship with me in the transference and the distance between her persecuting devil-mother in the provinces and her idealized father-God in the heavens. To give an example, her first dream in the first month of her analysis was as follows: *'I am watching a horrible scene of being on a station with no platform. In dreams, there are never platforms. There are many railway lines so I go to ask the porter where to catch the train. He is French and laughs at me and then punches my ticket full of holes.'* She then says that the analyst is the porter laughing at her and by destroying her ticket he is preventing her from going to see her father. Her father had written to her the previous day to come home for a couple of days as her mother was ill. The patient does not really want to go and accept responsibility for missing sessions and so she wants me to stop her. (She can associate and interpret her dream a little in this way as she had had some previous psychotherapy.) I then asked why she described the scene as horrible since I as the foreign porter was preventing her from missing the sessions as she apparently wished me to do. She then said 'The rest of the dream is horrible', and told me a long detailed account of her mental hospital and the patients being all ready to blow it up, while she herself was murdering a child. She was feeling as though all this might be real and had no associations to it. I then interpreted that she might well be concerned about my response to her missing her sessions but I also thought that she was very anxious about the journey that her analysis represents, that she doesn't know of the starting point, the platform, that she doesn't know what line to take and how I will respond to her not knowing; she is also terrified that it will lead her to destructive activities in this mental hospital and so she has to murder the growing child in herself that might become dependent on me. She replied that she was terrified of these feelings coming out of her. This indicates the way that such dreams, which are so borderline in experience and so lacking in much associative material, need to be interpreted; that one has to do a great deal of direct symbolic interpretation in order to see what meaning this might have for the patient and to indicate to the patient in these early stages of treatment that the analyst, at least, believes that dreams have meanings. The interpretations are aimed at conveying the immediate here-and-now emotional relationship between the patient and analyst in the context of the sessional occurrences. In addition, one may have to interpret the function of the dream for these patients as described by Segal (1981), particularly when it is felt that the dream is not being used as a vehicle for the communication of psychic states but as one for the evacuation of such states.

By the end of the two years, the situation in the analysis had altered. She realized reluctantly that she was indeed very ill and that she really needed me and the analysis if she wanted to recover, and it was now that she entered a phase of transference psychosis where she experienced me not only as the helpful, needed, and idealized analyst but also as the persecuting, murderous devil-mother or male agent of this mother. She was in a state of terror and partial ego-fragmentation for much of the time. The important point for our present concern is that her experience of her dreams changed too. She now fully realized that her dreams were only dreams and not the concrete reality of symbolic substitution processes, and, equally important, she no longer felt as though she were in a cinema or theatre being the passive onlooker of distant events. Instead she felt very involved and at times almost overwhelmed by events in the dream, often struggling furiously with them. There would still sometimes be two of her but both were now actively involved. At times she had such panic from this experience of being overwhelmed that she would awaken from them in an anxiety state; occasionally she found it difficult to get out of her dream state when she awoke so that her awake reality-aware state was almost overwhelmed by the dream state. Clinically she was now much more involved in working at and using her dreams to gain insight into her condition.

Over the course of several months, this transference psychosis phase was worked through and we entered the third phase, that of the transference neurosis. By this time she had almost become a whole person with a fairly firm grasp of reality. Her bizarre delusions, the depersonalization and derealization, had disappeared; she had developed a good sense of self and was now able to tolerate moderately depressive feelings without regressing into a paranoid and split state. We were left with the task of resolving her urinary disturbance and associated sexual inhibitions. Now once more her experiencing of her dreams changed. Instead of the 'ego-distancing dreams' of the first stage, or the 'ego-overwhelming dreams' of the second stage, as I call them, she now had the sort of dream experience that most people have, the type I formerly described. She was either watching, or being bothered, or anxious, or experiencing freedom, but she was not restricted to any single type of experience as a regular occurrence. On the whole, her experiencing was of a tolerable participating kind, which involved the new integration of her ego with its improved functioning in both the intrapsychic and interpersonal spheres as seen and experienced in the dream and in the transference.

I now want to look at the theoretical model that would help in the understanding of these changes in dream experiencing. The 'ego-distancing dreams' are based on the primitive psychic mechanisms of the splitting-off and denial of unwanted parts of the self and the projection of them into distant objects (a form of projective identification), and then passively watched. These mechanisms are reflected in the transference relationship of that phase with the additional feature that she is passively watching me in the act of actively watching and 'spying' on her. As the analytic work proceeds and she eventually is able to lessen the extent of these mechanisms and really accept that she is ill and needs me as a helpful, albeit idealized object, the distanced persecutory and idealized objects are accepted back into the consulting room, into the analyst and into the patient, and the overwhelming experiences represent her struggle and anxiety to contain them and to resist being taken over, particularly by her own devilish and murderous impulses. This struggle, however, is now taking place in an environment where the analyst, by his management of the case, is acting as a holding (to use Winnicott's term) and containing (to use Bion's term) object for the anxieties and impulses of this potentially ego-overwhelming situation.

The experience of the ego-distancing dream where the patient feels that she is in a cinema or theatre clearly has affinities with Bertram Lewin's concept of the dream-screen (1946). He thought that all dreams were projected onto a screen which is occasionally visible, and he suggested that the screen is a symbol of both sleep and the fusion of the ego with the breast with which sleep is unconsciously equated, albeit in a flat, two-dimensional form. He thought that the visual imagery of the dream represented wishes that would disturb the state of sleep. Charles Rycroft (1951) in a paper on the dream-screen thought that it was not present in all dreams but was a phenomenon that occurred in the dreams of patients who were entering a manic phase. For him, it symbolized the manic sense of ecstatic fusion with the breast and a denial of hostility towards it. I would agree with Rycroft that the dream-screen is not present in all dreams and that it can symbolize fusion with the breast and denial of hostility towards it, but I am not so sure about the manic sense of ecstatic fusion. I could detect no affect in the patient that would suggest a sense of ecstasy. I would postulate that in addition to fusion and denial of hostility towards the breast, the screen also represents the desire for a breast (mother) who can survive, contain, and take care of the unwanted projected aspects of the self.

I also want to relate these concepts not only to the dream-screen but also to the concept of dream-space, put forward by Masud Khan in 1973 in a Symposium held at a Scientific Meeting of The British Psycho-Analytical Society on the Role of Dreams in Psychoanalysis (Khan 1974). Also at this Symposium Segal presented her paper on atypical dreams, which outlined her views of the function of dreams, and I presented the views here outlined on the experience of dreams and the transference. It was interesting that, quite independently, these three papers all dealt with dreams experienced in severely disturbed patients and the ways in which they differed from dreams as previously described and conceptualized. To quote from Khan's paper:

> I wish also to distinguish the concept of dream-space from Bertram Lewin's instructive concept of dream-screen. The dream-screen is

something on to which the dream imagery is projected, whereas the dream-space is a psychic area in which the dream process is actualised into experiential reality. The two are distinct psychic structures, though complementary to each other.

(Khan 1974: 314)

I agree with this and also wonder whether a further way of regarding the dream-screen and the dream-space is that they represent psychic structures in a continuum of development of dreaming experience from a two- to a three-dimensional stage. Segal, in her paper, put forward the concept that 'the psychic space of the dream ultimately derives from the breast containing projective identification, not a dream-screen in terms of Lewin but a dream container' (1973: 13). I would suggest that the dream-screen represents a breast that is wished for but has never been adequately experienced as able to contain the projective identifications, whereas the dream container, from which she postulates that psychic space is derived, represents the analyst who can contain the projective identifications, associated emotions, and anxieties.

In addition to the concept of dream-space, Khan in his paper also presented his views on dream experience, which, although it is rather different from the one I am suggesting, similarly argues that a clear distinction needs to be made between the dream experience and the dream text on the basis of clinical experience.

In terms of clinical practice, these changes in dream experiencing constitute a valuable indication of real and potentially permanent psychic change in the patient in terms of the ego's capacity for growth and integration. They complement that other dream indicator of psychic change, the changes in the symbolic content in the manifest content of the dream. The observation of ego-distancing dreams in a patient is valuable in helping the assessment of the type and severity of the patient's psychopathology and of the types of defensive strategies that are in operation. Since the initial observations, I have observed these changes in a number of patients, usually severely hysterical, phobic, borderline schizoid, or psychotic personalities, who utilize primitive mental processes to an excessive degree. In some, I only observed the first and third stage and they did not seem to go through the ego-overwhelming stage; in others only the second and third stage were observable and not the first. Possibly particular sorts of psychopathology have different patterns of change or perhaps I have not been told of the complete experiences in a way that I could pick up.

A rather different approach to the idea of ego-distancing in dreams was made by E. Sheppard and L. Saul (1958) in a study of ego-function.

They used the manifest content of dreams for the study of ego activities, particularly unconscious activities. They differentiated ten categories of ego-functions and subdivided each category into four sub-groups, which listed different degrees of ego-awareness in dreams of impulses welling into the dream. Impulses were defined as urges, drives, needs, or other motivating forces expressed in the dream-scene. The more the dreamer portrayed his impulses as not being part of himself, the more he was said to be putting them at a distance from his ego, giving rise to the concept of 'ego-distancing'. They devised an 'ego rating system' to obtain some sort of quantitative assessment of this aspect of ego-functioning and demonstrated that the ego of psychotic patients showed greater variations in the number of defence mechanisms used in the manifest content than did those of the non-psychotic. The greatest degree of ego-distancing was obtained in the dreams of psychotic patients. They were able in fact to examine the dreams of persons unknown to them and then predict with a reasonable degree of accuracy whether the person was psychotic or not. However, the further development in patients from ego-distancing to ego-overwhelming dreams as a result of analysis is not described by them.

In 1976 in a paper given to the British Psycho-Analytical Society on the use of dreams in the analysis of a borderline, Athol Hughes described a sequence of dreams similar to the one that I had described. It is significant from her description of the clinical changes that the change from ego-distancing to ego-overwhelming dreams occurred when the patient acknowledged that the analyst was really needed and helpful for the analysis. This exactly tallies with my own clinical observation, as I have already described. In 1978 in a paper on dreaming and the organizing function of the ego, Cecily de Monchaux wrote of psychotics, and patients sometimes during analysis, feeling that their dreams threaten to take over and destroy the ego, which is clearly akin to the concept of ego-overwhelming. In 1981, I described a more extensive series of dream-experience changes that I observed in the analysis of a psychotic patient which were again mirrored by changes in his transference experience and it is to this that I now wish to turn.

The patient came to see me some years ago feeling suicidal after his girlfriend had left him. The reason he gave for feeling suicidal was that he felt he had become her, a woman, even though he was aware he had a man's body. When after a few sessions he told me that he had been born a girl but had then changed into a boy, and also believed he was God, I realized that I had a psychotic patient on my hands. He fitted somewhere in the description of transsexualism as described by Adam

Limentani (1979), displaying the features described by him of profound early disturbance of symbol formation and phantasies of fusion. In the transference the patient did not experience himself and myself as two persons being together in a room. As far as he was concerned experientially, no one existed in my room and neither did the room. What he did experience was the concrete phantasy of his mind being a ball with a hole in the top through which came the voice of the analyst, the whole existing in a void. Any other feelings were experienced as being 'a million miles away'. It has taken many years of analysis for him almost to accept that bodies and feelings exist and are real. He has remained at work during the whole of his analysis so far and in a social setting he would appear to be mentally normal although he has few relationships with others; his psychosis has remained relatively encapsulated.

At first he did not dream at all or, at least, he did not report any dreams. When he did, he was always the onlooker in ego-distancing dreams but had no associations to them. For him, the dream was its manifest content and that was that. They were not experienced completely as reality for they were still dreams, although he felt that they did not belong to him in the sense of being psychic experience but rather occurred as a world in which he could live. When I tried to offer him possible meanings of the dream in terms of symbolic content, relating the content to the contextual background of material, or suggesting their evacuating function, he mocked and derided such statements as rubbish. He lacked the capacity to progress from the symbolic equation to the symbol. Furthermore, to accept that his conscious processes were not only what they appeared to be but also contained different meanings which were being understood by someone other than himself was too bitter a pill for his God-like, supremely omniscient and omnipotent narcissism.

Gradually he began to associate to his dreams and as a result of working with the interconnections between dream and transference interpretations, particularly his omnipotent narcissism, he began to accept the feeling of the woman being inside him instead of being terrified of it. This was shown by various aspects of his behaviour while lying on the couch, an activity that he enjoyed as being feminine. He now believed that he was two people, a man and a woman, and that I was the voice of either his mother or his father. He then started to have the frightening experience of dreaming two dreams simultaneously. To give an example, he dreamed that *his parents were old, ill, and distressed, which in fact they were, and that he felt very sorry for them, while at the same time he was also dreaming that he was a monster gloating over his parents'*

37

misfortunes. He was afraid that having (what I would call) these 'split dreams' meant that he was going mad and he hated to see the frightening, gloating monster as himself, and obviously, the parents also referred to the analyst. The interest of this phenomenon of the split dream is that he had these dreams after he had been able to accept the split in himself and in the analyst into two people. The interpersonal transference relationship was followed by an intrapsychic change as shown by the dreams.

I certainly wondered what was happening in his psychic apparatus and processes to enable him to have two dreams simultaneously, even though they were related by content, as the example demonstrates. Could the dreaming processes really split into two parts to provide two dreams simultaneously? As I have been unable to find any reference to such dreams in the literature, I was unable to give an answer to my question at that time, but the answer came via a different form of dream experience some months later and, once again, it occurred only after a change in his relationship with me. He came to a session saying he was angry with me, although he still felt frozen solid, and the reason for his anger was that I had made him change. The change was that he used to see his family, himself, and myself as a conglomerate whole but now they were becoming separate people instead of a conglomeration. This recognition of the idea of separateness was followed by a split dream, in which *the patient was on a boat seeing a woman being raped by a man, whilst simultaneously dreaming that the woman was a man being raped by another man.* The significant aspect for this discussion is not the interpretation of the dream but his realization on awakening from sleep that he had, in fact, had two dreams, one following the other, and that he had telescoped them into one, a form of conglomeration. This then explained the apparent splitting of the dreaming processes and this realization had followed the recognition of separateness in the transference.

Some months after this, he told me that his suicidal feelings had gone and this fact depressed him. I suggested that it was depressing for him to have to acknowledge that I was a separate and useful analyst. This was followed by his first ego-overwhelming dream, 'overwhelming' being the word he spontaneously used, and I knew that he did not read the psychoanalytical literature in which he might have seen my first dream paper. He felt it was overwhelming as he was afraid of the dream taking over his mind, which it had done for most of the day, and that he would then be unable to distinguish fact from dream. He had never wanted to acknowledge any difference between internal and external reality, and so I believe that the reason for his anxiety was that he felt that he would have no control over the psychic reality of his dreams as he felt that he had over his waking psychic reality, and this would mean that the analyst might take over his mind. It should again be noted that the change from ego-distancing to ego-overwhelming dreams occurred after the patient had really acknowledged the presence of the helpful and needed analyst.

Shortly after this he expressed his fear of discovering that dreams are only dreams and not a world that he could live in, and that he and I would both have bodies and be together and separate in a consulting room. This was immediately followed by his first-ever three-dimensional dream of a vivid intensity, and this both excited and scared him. His fear was of his discovery of space and spatial relationships and all that this might mean to him in terms of growth, mobility, and freedom, and he then realized that he had always compressed space into a tight flatness to make it two-dimensional, like the dream-screen of the ego-distancing type of dreams, in order to avoid this frightening situation. Once again the further interpersonal realizations of separateness, of bodies existing in the space of a room, were followed by the discovery of intrapsychic dream-space, the three-dimensional dream experience. The analysis still continues.

In view of the fact that these changes in dream experience are always preceded by changes in the transference relationship, support is lent to the position that it is from the development of the external interpersonal relationships in the transference, where experiences of space, mobility, and separateness arise, that internalization of these processes and experiences occur to give rise to experiences of internal space, mobility, and separateness as manifested in these dream experiences. It is in the context of the constant interchange between these external and internal processes that growth and positive psychic change occur. The real acknowledgement by the patient of the analyst's helpfulness, skill, and reliability for the needs of the patient is an essential and vital factor for the facilitation of these changes.

I will summarize these changes of transference experience and the associated dream experience:

1	Almost no reality of patient and analyst	ego-distancing dreams, almost concretely real
2	Acceptance of both patient and analyst as two gender entities	simultaneous split dreams
3	Part-separation of patient and analyst	simultaneous dreams become consecutive

4	Acknowledgement of helpful analyst	ego-overwhelming dreams
5	Acknowledgement of patient's and analyst's physical reality	three-dimensional dreams, which are now not reality

Note

1 First version published in the *International Journal of Psycho-Analysis*, 1973, 54: 345–7 and the *International Journal of Psycho-Analysis*, 1981, 62: 301–7.

Changes in the experiencing of inner space[1]

The origin of this topic was a remark made to me by a patient towards the latter part of her analysis. 'You know', she said, 'that the empty space I've always felt inside has changed. It's become a real space and feels so different.' From the beginning of her treatment, one of her main complaints had been of an empty space inside herself which she hated, at least as much as it was possible for her to feel hate, and compulsively tried to fill by eating and sexual promiscuity, neither of which gave anything other than a temporary respite to her emptiness. The change in her inner spatial experience was the herald of potential satisfaction and gratification and it is to the elaboration of this change, together with this potential, that I wish to address myself.

I was interested in my patient's statement and so I wanted to find out what other analysts had written about it. To my surprise there is very little written on the topic of inner space. The only paper specifically dealing with it is by J. Grotstein (1978), 'Inner space: its dimensions and its coordinates', but it is mainly concerned with theoretical issues. Other than his, the only references are in Marion Milner's book, *The Hands of the Living God* (1969). There is, of course, a great deal written about external space, and there are many references to other forms of space, such as psychic space, potential space (Winnicott 1971), dream space (Khan 1974); Bion (1967) speaks of the container as a component of psychic space, and Grotstein in his paper also speaks of emotional space, rational space, ultimate space, moral space, negative space, and transitional space. The space issue I am addressing is an experiential one, whereas much of the literature refers to theoretical concepts not necessarily based on spatial experience in any way.

The notion of inner space is however intimately bound up with that of emptiness; yet surprisingly even here, M. Singer, in his papers 'The experience of emptiness in narcissistic and borderline states: I and II' (1977), remarks that 'the psychoanalytical literature is surprisingly meagre in its dealing with the subjective disturbance of emptiness'.

41

Pertinent to the issues in this paper are a chapter in Kernberg's (1975) book *Borderline Conditions and Pathological Narcissism* called 'On the subjective experience of emptiness', and a paper by Winnicott, 'Fear of breakdown' (1974), and I shall turn to this after I have given an account of the analysis of my patient which is appropriate to these issues.

The analysis

Miss J. was referred to me by a colleague with whom she had been in analysis for about five years. Her reasons for seeking help initially were that she felt depressed and had some conflict over her homosexual feelings. It soon became clear that more fundamentally she was out of touch with her feelings, and her analyst thought she could best be described as suffering from a narcissistic disorder. By this term, her analyst meant a disorder in which 'psychological problems centred on an insufficiently consolidated self on the one hand but where the self has attained a certain cohesiveness on the other. In this one can observe the essential difference between borderline and narcissistic pathology. Borderline patients can be said not to have a cohesive self' (quotation from an unpublished paper on this patient in the Scientific Bulletin of the British Society). During the course of her first analysis, the patient made considerable improvement and she was referred to me when her analyst retired from practice.

When I first met Miss J., I saw an attractive woman of about thirty. It did not take many sessions before I realized that she was not so much a woman as a well-bred Girl Guide, artistic and intellectually minded in an arty-crafty manner. I also realized that she was dowdy; she always wore the same clothes and this was not for lack of means. It was a reflection of part of her psychopathology, since she was quite out of touch with her femininity, and more importantly, wished never to change anything, a wish that clearly conflicted with a successful outcome to an analysis. This was one of the reasons why at her first interview she told me she was a fraud and a charlatan. She also told me that her words and actions didn't connect with her feelings; if she did have feelings about a situation, they might be experienced but only some time after the event. She had never had an experience of spontaneity. The coming retirement of her analyst was making no impact on her but she knew she would experience it later and then regret not having done so earlier.

She spoke a little of confusion existing among the females of her family and said that her father was somewhere around. We decided that she would enter analysis with me after the retirement but that it would have to be on a three-times-a-week basis for a while. During the waiting period, she wrote asking me to remember her other two sessions, saying, 'September onwards feels a bit like this', and she drew a sketch of a girl falling through the meshes of a large net, adding, 'I really just mean that the holes or gaps in the net seem large enough to enable escape – even if it is from myself'.

She worked in a job far below the talents she had but was unable to use. During the first weeks I received some impression of how she operated. There was the split between words and actions and her feelings, already mentioned. Her voice always sounded bland and a little metallic; she once described it as a 'fizzy monotone' which was very apt. It went with a use of language that was engaging and interesting since metaphor played a large part. She reminded me of Virginia Woolf without the acid. The sound of her voice together with the content of her speech was one of her ways in which she could both excite my imagination and yet also clog it – the fizziness and the monotony. She apparently conformed to what other people expected of her and endeavoured to mould herself to these expectations by her sensitivity to their moods, to such an extent that she felt she had no separate existence. Yet at the same time, she also made secret and devious attacks upon people by not saying, even when asked, what she did or did not want in order to make others decide for her and so make them irritated. She also attacked expectations by failing in everything: 'I doom everything to failure.' These activities were partly manifestations of her desires and anxieties concerning fusion and separation from her objects. In the transference they were shown in the way she dealt with interpretations or any potential advance that could arise from insight. She would make my interpretations her own, work with them for a time and then drop them to doom them to failure. 'Go away' was one of her favourite phrases yet at the same time she dreaded the breaks between sessions. She longed to feel as though she were in a warm bath, never having to do anything or feel anything more than a warm state of fusion.

The breaks between sessions and even more the weekend and holiday breaks were experienced as severe deprivations, during which she felt that everything had been drained from her, leaving her empty and exhausted. 'I'm a stick-insect,' she said. She had a boyfriend whom she used as a replacement for me, and if he were unavailable, would stay in her rented lodging-room, sitting on the floor, burning incense, watching TV, and compulsively eating hard cheese. 'I eat everyone,' she said, to try to assuage her emptiness and cut-off feelings at the breaks.

She described the feeling of emptiness as having an empty space inside her that was hollow and resonant, that wanted to be filled but never could be no matter how much she tried. As well as this, she also had an outer space experience: 'I feel as if I'm living in a private space capsule with empty space all around it.' Not only was her inner space empty but also her outer space, apart from the private space capsule. These feelings in her were reflected by my experience of her in the counter-transference. She would interest me with her metaphorical talk and ideas but I would then find that I felt bored, that my interest had wandered and that I was no longer with her. The 'fizzy monotony' was affecting me; the metaphors feeding me and attempting to fill the monotony, the underlying emptiness. Kernberg describes this counter-transference feeling as mirroring a state in the patient which he calls 'schizoid emptiness', and this is to be differentiated from a different state of emptiness, that he calls 'depressive emptiness'. I shall come to this later.

Early in the analysis, the interpretation that made most impact on her was my saying that she seemed to have no sense of self, of an I or me. Because of this lack of a self, it seemed that all external stimuli or demands were experienced as impingements, to use Winnicott's phrase, on whatever sense of going-on-being she possessed; perhaps even worse, all internal stimuli, such as thoughts, feelings, phantasies, and bodily needs, were similarly experienced. Under these circumstances, her desire for a warm bath life would be one in which she hoped to escape from all stimuli. This desire would also accord with Balint's (1952) concept of a state of primary object love in which there is an absolute harmony between the subject and the environment with no interference whatsoever from any source either external or internal. She existed on a false-self basis protecting whatever might exist of her true or real self. To use a Kleinian theoretical framework, any aspect of the self as far as there is one, which would disturb this harmonious state, would have to be projected into the environment, and the now-emptied self would have to fit around and identify with these projections in an attempt to recapture the harmony. My own diagnosis of the patient is that she was borderline rather than narcissistic in structure in view of her lack of a sense of self.

However, this was not simply a solipsistic universe that the patient had created for herself from her own internal needs; she had a family history and background to account for much of this dynamic. She came from a family whose social position derived mainly from her mother's side. Her father was a successful self-made man upon whom her mother looked down, both as a social inferior since he was self-made, and as occupationally inferior since he was a business man. Her mother, together with her two daughters – my patient and her sister – formed an intellectual, artistic, and do-gooding circle in the family from which her father, 'the faithful sheepdog', 'the clumsy oaf', was excluded. He in his turn fitted into his family role by excluding himself from most of the family conversations and discussions by retiring into his study to smoke, read, or listen to music. It took a long time before she was prepared to realize that her despised father was in fact the provider and maintainer of this almost royal female circle.

In the female family circle, nothing could be mentioned that might in any way diminish the near-perfection of the family; any imperfections in personal relationships were always located as outside the family. No words or expressions of anger, jealousy, envy, disappointments were allowed to be spoken of as existing between one member of the family and another. Her father's existence was the only disturbance of this family romance and was the only family source of disturbance that her mother would allow into the circle. She could do no other as she had chosen him to be her husband. However, her mother had also introduced another, more serious, disturbance into the family and this was in the shape of malignant disease. Since Miss J.'s childhood, her mother had suffered on and off from cancer, requiring regular treatment. It had been noted that recurrences of the cancer had often coincided with any emotional upset or crisis in the family and this provided an unspoken weapon of terrifying proportions against any member of the family contemplating disturbing the family status quo. For the patient, it meant that her phantasies and feelings of her destructive omnipotence were most powerfully reinforced by this reality and much analytic work was done to enable her to distinguish the phantasy from the reality. When she discovered that minor illnesses or low moods of mine that she perceived did not develop into malignancies or severe illnesses in the face of her phantasies, it was very reassuring to her.

This family constellation was a clear external factor in the patient's grandiosity and omnipotence and also in her feelings of helplessness and of not wanting anything to change. But together with her recognition of lack of sense of self, we became more fully aware of her intense envy of others. This was particularly directed towards those around her who were leading useful or successful lives and she also felt shocked to discover the extent of her *schadenfreude*. She began to feel ill, sleepy and depressed, couldn't be bothered to tidy her room, and lived on a diet of bread, cheese, and television. She was afraid that her depression, which she called 'a sort of madness', would be too much for me and give me a cancer or something similar. Because of this, she wanted me to 'sod off' since she saw me as a troublemaker in expecting her to be real and not just falsely nice, and yet envied and felt vicious about my ability to understand and help her. To try and escape from this, she felt she wasn't really involved in the depression but that she and I were watching someone with her name being depressed. By this time my counter-transference feelings were of her being in the room with me much of the time and she felt a little more real.

She now began to tell me about her sexual phantasies. I already knew that her body had no value for her; almost any man could have it and so give it some temporary worth to her. She had practically no pleasure in sexual intercourse but did acknowledge some perverse types of gratification. She was 'fixed' to an experience when she was seven years old of watching boys urinate into bottles; this had excited her, making her wish she could have been a boy. She now had phantasies of tying up men, giving them an erection with her hands and of having them ejaculate over her body. In practice, it was restricted to ejaculation over her abdomen without tying up her partner. She saw the connection between semen and urine, her identification with both the boy and the bottle and her masochistic pleasure at the humiliation of feeling peed on. It could be seen in the transference as tying me into knots and using the interpretations I gave as superficial urine to humiliate her pleasurably rather than as semen that could fertilize her and nourish growth as in proper sexual intercourse.

The full realization now came to her of not wanting to change in analysis and soon after this she made her first spontaneous statement to me – 'Stop putting your big foot in it,' she said when I made a wrong interpretation. This was soon followed by an awareness of a 'me' inside herself that was terrified by the way she was shutting out her life from being lived. Her real self was now appearing on the scene. She revealed that she had long had a deeply held conviction that she had everyone trapped and under her control; any perception that might contradict this was angrily rejected and told to go away. This was the very stuff of a delusion. It was now my turn to perceive and understand something about her. I started to appreciate that almost always she lay on the couch with one arm behind her head and I now wondered if it represented anything more than comfort. We worked out that it represented being held in her mother's arms, a way of keeping her thoughts private, of keeping out unwanted, interfering perceptions, of preventing me from seeing what was happening inside her, and of depriving me of any voyeuristic pleasure that I might obtain in the process. It also formed for her the private space-capsule previously mentioned. Following this she was able to move her hand from her head in a natural, not a forced, way, thereby giving up one of her non-verbal defences.

The theme of non-verbal communication was important in helping Miss J. to understand certain aspects of her family's pathology. She had

46

told me early on that at school she had been given a nickname that reflected her habits of peering and prying into other people's affairs, and it became clear that she did this both in her analysis and in the family setting. One of the objects of her secret prying was to watch for any signs of discord between others and, if observed, she secretly gloated over them. She had, for example, noticed that her mother had a characteristic gesture of her shoulder towards her father, the equivalent of the cold shoulder. She noticed how her father's partial deafness could suddenly become more acute if necessary or how his withdrawals from the family circle could become more frequent. We gradually built up the picture of how the family members' hostility to one another was communicated by non-verbal gestures in symbolic behaviour. These observations and seeing them at work in the transference – as, for example, by excluding me with her arm or cold-shouldering me – was a great relief to her as again it helped her to be aware that open expressions of hostility were not as damaging as she feared.

Her experience of living her life now commenced. She started to have feelings of being real, with her emotions connecting with her words and actions. With an unpleasant shock she realized that she had never actually cared about other people unless they had behaved in ways that she had wanted, as with any show of independence of spirit, her caring was withdrawn. In this way she was repeating the family pattern; she well appreciated the ruthlessness behind the family's do-gooding values, and realized that in the analytic setting she had been exposed to something different, in that both analysts had respected her own wishes and individuality without withdrawing concern for her. She felt very strongly that she now had to choose between these two ways of caring and knew that if she chose the family model, she might just as well give up her analysis. On the other hand, she knew that if she chose the analyst's path, she would have to face all her fears involved in giving up her techniques of eating, fusing with, and becoming other people. After this, it came as a great surprise to her to discover that her thoughts were really her own and quite private and not in possession of others unless she chose to disclose them.

Next she found herself a room of her own. She gave up her squalid lodging-room and bought an attractive flat with a garden, something she had always thought about but never dared have. She discovered the existence of external space and also of time, and now those bodily sensations that previously had only been unpleasant impingements and demands became pleasurable and exciting. These sensations also involved her sexual organs which she had perviously left untouched, and being in some ways a methodical girl, she bought numerous books

47

on female sexuality, and, with their use, explored herself and particularly the various forms of genital masturbation. She even bought a mechanical vibrator for optimal exploration and this, together with her hands, took her on her journey into her inner space, finding it accompanied by a quality of being real and potentially fulfilling. However, she also found that although clitoral stimulation was very exciting, it also produced lesbian urges which made her feel rather mad because of the intensity with which she wanted to have her own penis. Soon intense disappointment at not having a penis set in, and this together with a fading of the anti-depressant-like aspects of the masturbation led to the return of the feelings of emptiness and depression. She felt that I had pressurized her into a business-like way of ordering things to change her life-style; in this I was felt to resemble her father who would take over any project she might mention to him with his efficient, business-like expertise in his over-enthusiasm to be helpful to his daughter, yet she simultaneously recognized that I had not behaved like that but had allowed her to discover and do things for herself. For herself, she believed that one of the most important findings of this period was to discover that if she looked at her life from the vantage point of her having been very ill and depressed without knowing it, it made complete sense in explaining to her why nothing previously had either real meaning or significance for her, leaving her feeling just an empty shell.

The depression and emptiness deepened and she began to feel suicidal and worried that she might actually kill herself. It also made her anxious to think of the effect such feelings might make on her mother's cancer and also of their possible effects on me. My counter-transference in this period was one of concern, interest, and involvement with her and much aware of the depressed atmosphere but at no time did I become really anxious about the suicidal risk. This present state of emptiness and depression in the patient corresponds to Kernberg's 'depressive emptiness', and in this case, the two states of emptiness, schizoid and depressive, have followed in sequence during the course of the analysis.

She saw the Woody Allen film *Interiors*, which portrays among other things a suicidal mother, and this gave her what she called the bizarre idea that it was the cancer that was keeping her mother alive. At first I found this a puzzling notion, but after thinking about it I suggested to her that her mother might have felt suicidal before the development of her cancer, that the cancer would have alleviated these suicidal feelings in that she really did suffer from something internally that might kill her; I suggested that her mother had perhaps been left with a more mild, secondary depression as a reaction to the effects of the cancer. I also suggested that if her cancer were cured, the suicidal feelings might return. These suggestions, she said, made absolute sense to her. The actual experience of feeling suicidal herself and then of discovering a suicidal mother with whom she had identified early in life was of the utmost importance to her. It resulted in her feeling better, fuller, and less greedy for food, together with the change of her inner experience of 'empty space' into 'real space'.

Gradually the depression lifted and her sexual phantasies came intensely to the fore again. She phantasized that I was masturbating in my chair, that she was masturbating me, or that I was on top of her but not penetrating her. She found that phantasizing was more exciting than actual sex play with a man as it paradoxically made her feel more real. Her most intense desire was to be a man and she became obsessed with penis-like objects, so much so that she became afraid of silences in the analysis since she felt afraid she might uncontrollably put her hand on my penis. Yet this immediately led her to the feeling that she was now far more in control of herself and her surroundings. One way this showed itself was in her attitude to money. Previously she had spent it without thought as it had no value or meaning but now she was beginning to appreciate its value and to recognize that there was no magical, everlasting source of it. However, she did not appreciate finding out that she had always been an indiscreet gossip.

At this time she started to go out with a man she had known distantly for some years but with whom she had never had any sexual contact. It was no surprise for me to learn that previously he had had mainly homosexual attachments. During an analytic break, without any discussion in the analysis, she became engaged to him but in spite of the clear acting-out, it soon became evident that she had made a good choice. He proved that he was no passive bisexual whose penis she was to possess absolutely, but a man with a mind of his own, a very caring attitude towards her, and a good lover. She was anxious about her marriage, as her mother had been upset and developed a recurrence of her cancer when the patient's sister had married, but nevertheless she went ahead and her fears were not realized. She idealized her marital state, seeing herself and her husband as babes-in-the-wood, but naturally the cracks in the idealization soon began to appear. One of the most important concerned her husband's previous homosexuality, since she started to indulge in an exciting phantasy of her husband and another man making love to each other. She became anxious that her own sexual demands on him would drive him to return to his homosexuality and in being demanding she could be attempting to actualize her phantasy. However, she now felt confident enough to discuss these real issues with him and this resulted in a strengthening of the bond between them. She soon became pregnant and was both delighted and anxious, particularly at their having to be real parents and not the babes-in-the-wood.

Unfortunately the analysis now had to end. We both knew that her problems, particularly the sexual ones, remained unresolved but that she could manage with the help she had received from her analysis, and it is clear that her existential state is very different from the one that she had when she first sought analytic help.

Discussion

We can now proceed to a discussion of inner space and the associated emptiness as they manifest themselves in the analysis. It is clear that the two experiences are intimately related and can only be separated for consideration in a rather arbitrary fashion. The patient spoke of an 'empty space' which changed into a 'real space', but the questions arise, first, what would constitute an empty space as against a real space, and second, whether the distinction being made by the patient was simply idiosyncratic to her or had more general relevance. I believe that my patient was making a genuine distinction between the two experiences of inner space and that we need to understand this distinction in already existing psychoanalytical formulations so far as we are able.

1 Inner space

As I mentioned at the beginning of this chapter, there is a great paucity of references to the experience of an inner space but, for my purposes, the work of Marion Milner has been very fruitful. In her book, previously referred to, Milner has given us an account of the psycho-analysis of a severely schizoid young woman in which the drawings made by that patient during her treatment were a vital part of the communications made to her analyst, since the analyst was able to use them in her inimitable creative way. She considered the drawings in relation to her idea of inner space:

> Slowly, as a result of pondering on these drawings and all she had said, I was to come to formulate a central question: does what was originally the on-going background of darkness and rhythmic beat of the mother's heart and breathing become, in later states of development, the inner awareness of one's own body? And if so,

how? Certainly her drawings so far had suggested that there must be a slow creating of a concept of an inner containing space, whatever may be the different materials of memory out of which it is built.

(Milner 1969: 122)

She goes on to discuss these different materials of memory:

I was to come to think of the experiences of that inner space that can be actively explored long before the hands can become explorers, the space that is one's mouth that can be explored with one's tongue. ... I even began to wonder whether the capacity to explore one's own inner space, by directing attention inwards to various parts of it, does not have its first bodily prototype in the exploring tongue that plays with, actively samples and relishes, the sense of the solidity of the nipple within one's mouth.

(1969: 123)

She changes the libidinal area: 'as showing how the whole conflict could have been transferred from the inner space of the mouth to the inner space of the rectum' (p.124). Further on:

Also I had been interested in more internal aspects of the frame; that is, in learning how to achieve concentrated states of mind in which one creates one's own inner frame, frame of reference, as essential in all mental productivity, whether creating ideas or works of art, a state in which one holds a kind of inner space; but I had not yet seen that one of the earliest roots of such a capacity might be the experience of being held in one's mother's arms.

(1969: 250)

Lastly:

But I thought that for Susan to achieve this becoming incarnate, thus separating herself off from mother-me, claiming the right to be 'behind her eyes' again, claiming her own point of view which could not be identical with anyone else's, for her such an act of affirming and claiming her own privacy within her skin could be felt as an ultimate selfishness, one that would bring annihilating retaliation from mother-me-the-world. What she could not see, or only intellectually, was that in fact such an affirming of her own private inner space, far from cutting her off from people, would in fact become the only basis for a true relationship to them.

(1969: 272)

51

From these quotations, it is evident that Milner's patient has similarities to mine; both are young, female, suffering from severe schizoid problems, operating on a false-self basis, and needing to be helped to find their real selves and their own private outer and inner space. It may well be that these problems of finding such space made my patient see her experiences in terms of inner space rather than emptiness. Milner gives five components in the creation of inner space: (i) the mouth, tongue, and nipple; (ii) the hands; (iii) the rectum; (iv) the mother's arms; (v) the ability to separate from the mother. If we look at my patient in terms of these components, there is evidence for each of them. For (i) there is the compulsive eating, and the preferred hard cheese could well be compared to an engorged nipple; for (ii) there is the exploration of her hands in her masturbation; for (iii) there is no direct evidence of rectal or bowel involvement but perhaps the problem with money is symbolically relevant here; for (iv) this was clearly very important for her in the creation of space; for (v) differentiation of herself from the suicidal mother resulted in the change of space from empty to real.

In addition to these five components described by Milner, I would like to add two more. The sixth component would be the vagina. Her exploration of herself with her hands and the vibrator into her sexual organs were vitally important to her in the discovery of her inner space and its functioning in the context of sexual excitation and orgasm. Following on from this would be the seventh component which could only be present in adulthood, and this would be the womb, sexual organs, and body in the processes of menstruation, pregnancy, and labour. The actual bodily changes inside the woman, the development of the foetus with its progressive quickening, movements of kicking, the process of delivery, and the immediate bodily changes following delivery must profoundly enrich a woman's experience of her inner space. Obviously, these two components must always be absent in the male experience of inner space.

Grotstein, in his 1978 paper, although being more concerned with different aspects of psychic space, does make some comments relevant for this chapter. He states:

I believe the capacity to experience space is a primary apparatus of ego autonomy in Hartmann's terms, which seems to have emerged from the inchoate sensations upon the foetal skin at birth, thereby 'awakening' the skin with its sense receptors into its functions as a surface, as a boundary between self and non-self, and as a container of self.

(1978: 56)

Also:

> I believe further that the development of the awareness and toler-
> ation of the 'gap', the space in distance and time between the going
> and coming of the primary object, constitutes the 'baptism' of space.
> If the infant can 'contain' this space in the absence of his object, he
> is able to initiate and expand his sense of space and is able therefore
> to be separate. Because of this he can perceive some separated aspects
> of his experience which then he can begin to represent.
>
> (1978: 56)

Grotstein's determinants of inner space, then, are (1) the skin, and (2)
the ability to separate from the mother. In the latter, he agrees with
Milner. I think that the skin determinant is evident from the patient's
desire to be in a warm bath, since this is precisely the situation in which
the functioning of the skin as a differentiating surface will be minimal.
E. Bick (1968) has also related the development of an internal space
that can hold and contain objects internally, with the experience of the
skin and its stimulation in the earliest mother–infant interaction.

The ability to separate from the mother would first be associated
with the experience of external space, the awareness of the gap
between the infant and its primary object. From this would follow the
internalization of this spatial relationship, which would constitute this
determinant for the experience of inner space. The ability to separate
in the analytic relationship is potentiated by the various factors in the
analytic setting. The limits of sessions in time, the breaks between
sessions, the spatial dimensions of the consulting room and the couch,
the reliability of the analyst's presence and his techniques of management will all act as non-verbal determinants of separateness. I would
regard the experience of empty space, both external and internal, as of
a limitless nature with an absence of any boundaries, whereas that of
real space, both external and internal, would indicate the presence of
limits and boundaries.

Her first feeling of reality came after the first spontaneous gesture,
her exclamation that I should 'stop putting my big foot in it'. This
clearly has transferential reference to her father, in her descriptions of
him, and we should then note that this paternal experience indicates his
important function in being the object that comes between the infant
and its mother and in so doing helps the separation process. He, too,
has his place in being a determinant in this way for the development of
inner space.

To recapitulate, I have discussed nine determinants of the development of the capacity to experience inner space, which may possibly be
regarded as a primary apparatus of ego autonomy. These are:

1 Mouth, tongue, and nipple.
2 Skin.
3 Hands.
4 Rectum.
5 Mother's arms.
6 Ability to separate from mother.
7 Vagina.
8 Menstruation, pregnancy, and labour.
9 Father's active presence and penis.

2 Emptiness

Having examined the components in the development of the capacity to experience inner space, we must give some attention to that of emptiness. For this I will recapitulate briefly the clinical course of the analysis. The experience of empty space was there from the start, and this experience of hers was matched by my own in the counter-transference, tallying with Kernberg's description of schizoid emptiness. This experience can be extreme in some patients, eventually culminating in the psychotic's loss of the experience of inner emptiness when the patient has lost the experience of possessing a body and hence inner and outer emptiness fuse to become a void. The psychotic patient described in Chapter 3 did not experience himself and myself as two persons together in a room. For him no one existed in the room and neither did the room. He experienced the concrete phantasy of his mind being a ball with a hole in the top through which came my voice, and the whole existed in a void.

Following the analysis of some of her envy and grandiosity, my female patient became depressed and ill but felt a little more real. Her perverse sadistic sexual phantasies emerged, as did her delusion of her omnipotent control; the analysis of the position of her arms and its private space all led to her emergence from depression and the exploration of her genitals and vagina. Further emergence of her homosexuality and penis envy, together with the failure of her manic-like masturbation, led to her suicidal depressed feelings and the discovery of a suicidal mother. This occasioned the change to real space, where some of the emptiness was filled. This phase tallied with Kernberg's depressive emptiness since my counter-transference to her had also changed, and this depressive emptiness was clearly equivalent in many ways to the patient's real space.

This was soon followed by further changes that could be seen as the result of experiences of positive emptiness. Winnicott remarks in his (1974) paper that 'emptiness is a prerequisite for eagerness to gather in. Primary emptiness simply means: before starting to fill up. A considerable maturity is needed for this stage to be meaningful' (p.106). He also says that, 'When the patient can reach to emptiness itself and tolerate this state because of dependence on the auxiliary ego of the analyst, then taking in can start up as a pleasurable function' (p.107). This type of emptiness is equivalent to a healthy inner space. The changes in the analysis to demonstrate this were her imaginative use of phantasy and her gathering in of a husband and children to fill the real inner space.

In Singer's papers on emptiness, mentioned above, stress is laid on the suicidal aspect of the topic; indeed the second paper is also titled 'The struggle for a sense of self and the potential for suicide'. He also comments in this paper on emptiness from the point of view of the self:

> Only with the recent advances in psychoanalytic theorizing regarding defects in ego and narcissistic realms, especially in regard to object relations, combined with the increasing number of borderline patients suffering from disturbances in the sense of self, could emptiness be studied as a result of this ego defect, as well as the traditional position from instinct theory, as primarily due to an oral hungry longing for emotional supplies from the good mother, or from defences against this and other fantasy formation.
>
> (Singer 1977: 471)

The patient here described had abundant problems with her experiences of self, clearly had longings for emotional supplies from a good mother, and, equally clearly, was heavily defending against the frightening suicidal mother.

The discovery of her feelings and ideas of her mother being suicidal and the understanding that I gave her by my interpretation of the reasons for the mother's emotional changes in this respect enabled her feelings towards her mother to change. Instead of a schizoid idealization, they changed to a depressive concern for a suffering mother as a real and whole person for the first time. It was this experience of the shift from the schizoid to the depressive state between her and her mother which was the psychic food that really filled her empty space and enabled her inner space to feel real, in the way that she and her mother felt real. From this point of view schizoid emptiness is a defence against a frightening depressive emptiness.

I shall conclude with a diagram that will illustrate schematically the relationships that I have been attempting to clarify between inner space and emptiness.

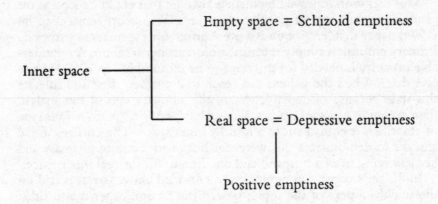

Note

1 First version published in the *International Journal of Psycho-Analysis*, 1985, 66: 255–64.

5

Levels of experiencing of thinking[1]

The issue that I want to explore here concerns changes in the experiencing of thoughts and thinking that I have observed clinically in the analysis of some patients. It will also concern the issue of consciousness that I previously examined, when exploring the hypnotic state. These are complex issues and I can touch only lightly upon them. I will be concentrating for my purposes solely on the theories of Freud and Bion and will be linking them to clinical observations made during the analysis of a schizophrenic patient.

We are all of us roughly aware of what we mean by ordinary thinking. We conceptualize ourselves as possessing something which we call 'a mind' and that we locate it as inside our head. We postulate the presence of this mind by the fact that we become aware of thoughts and perceptions which are then said to be a product of this mind's activity. These thoughts and perceptions are usually meaningful in some sequential type of way to us in that they serve as guides either to further lines of thought or to some physical activity. These thoughts and perceptions are said to be possessed of a property called 'psychical quality', which, to remind you, Freud (1895) in his Project described as

> sensations which are different in a great multiplicity of ways and whose difference is distinguished according to its relationship with the external world. Within this difference there are series, similarities, and so on, but there are in fact no quantities in it.

This possession of psychical quality allows thoughts to become conscious. We also know that this mind, by inference from clinical observations, has the property of unconscious thinking, of which by definition we are not aware, and that these unconscious thoughts do not possess the property of 'psychical quality'. The point I am stressing is that for normal or neurotic persons, thoughts which are in words and are then conscious possess a quality, a significance, a meaning for that person which he feels is a hallmark of normality of this aspect of mental

57

functioning which he calls 'thinking'. He may not, however, necessarily appreciate, to a greater or lesser degree, the significance of his thoughts.

The situation is rather different in persons suffering from the chronic psychoses, particularly schizophrenia, and I shall give as an example a young man who has been in analysis with me for several years and would bear the clinical psychiatric label of 'a case of chronic schizophrenia simplex'. He has always been able to talk to me in a fairly coherent fashion, even though I could not always be sure of the difference between fact and phantasy. He had the capacity to associate to his statements or dreams in the extraordinary way of many schizophrenics, in revealing the relationship of his statements to unconscious thoughts and motivations. But for him, as with other schizophrenic patients, the whole thing was meaningless as they were all isolated, empty statements, useless for any further thinking and useless as a guide for further action. He worked in a basic menial job and his thinking and activities were blind and automatic in response to external and internal situations and were associated with an almost complete lack of affect except for occasional panic attacks and a state of constant deep-seated unhappiness. On one occasion he said to me, 'The things I say have no meaning – they are like the froth on a glass of beer. I've got no consciousness of anything although it may seem from the way I talk that I have.'

As I have never experienced this state of mind myself, I find it very difficult to conceptualize or imagine the experience of what it must be like to exist in this state. The nearest I could come to it would be from an experience that is fairly common to most people. If we repeat to ourselves a word or a phrase over and over again, we notice after a time that the words have lost their meaning for us and we are left with the empty sound of the syllables. Perhaps this empty meaningless sound state spread over all our words is something comparable to the chronic schizophrenic state.

Let us examine the theoretical implications of this state. Freud (1900) postulated that the psychical system, consciousness, is the sense-organ for the perception of psychical quality, a topic I have discussed in the chapter on hypnosis. If the person has no perception himself of this quality – meaning and significance – apart from its absence, it can mean that the sense-organ is present but that the conditions for the production of psychical quality is absent, or that the sense-organ is lacking in some way and therefore quality cannot be perceived, or that both the sense-organ and psychical quality are absent. Freud (1915) in his paper on 'The unconscious' had further postulated that the condition necessary for things, objects, in the

58

unconscious to become conscious, or more strictly preconscious, was for the unconscious thing-presentation to be brought into contact with its preconscious word-presentation. He suggested that, in schizophrenia, libido is withdrawn from thing (object)-presentations and only the word-presentation of the thing (object) is cathected. From this, one can deduce that the presence or absence of psychical quality, meaning and significance, is dependent on the presence or absence of thing (object)-presentations being cathected with libido. To put this rather differently, for thoughts to have meaning and significance, there must be some sort of libidinal relationship to the object, both internally and externally.

The other possibility suggested for the lack of perception of quality was the absence of the perceptual system, consciousness. Bion (1957), as I have previously mentioned, suggested that in schizophrenia, parts of the perceptual apparatus could be split off and projected into objects, giving rise to bizarre objects. Since consciousness is regarded as a part of this perceptual system for the perception of psychical quality, it could be said that consciousness has been projected onto the analyst, who now by his observations and interpretations to the patient, is serving as the patient's consciousness, a concept I have previously used in discussing the functioning of the hypnotist. To anticipate a little, the recovery of the ability by the patient to have a conscious thought would then correspond to a re-introjection of this perceptual system back into the patient, modified by the analyst, and in the context of a feeding object relationship to be described.

Let us now return to the analysis. A few days before a Christmas break after a number of years of treatment, he told me during a session that on the previous evening he had had his first conscious thought for many years. This conscious thought had really meant something to him and he was very pleased to have had it. This thought was 'He was talking to me' (the 'he' being the analyst), and this thought had repeated itself several times over, but then he felt that it was being pulled back out of this conscious state and then it vanished. Since then, the thought had lost its meaning for him. Up till this event, there had been no conception of the analyst except as a vague force from somewhere behind him, but now the analyst had acquired the meaningful description of 'he'. It should be noted that this thought – he did not consider any of his previous communications to me to have been thoughts – was essentially a passive one of the analyst having done something to the patient. Since most of his communications were oral or symbolically oral in nature and content, this thought would indicate the presence of a fairly satisfying symbolic feeding relationship between analyst and patient.

The other feature of this relationship is that this thought had occurred just before a fairly lengthy separation, the Christmas break. It might have been thought that the last thing the patient would have wanted at this time would be a meaningful relationship with a departing object, which would leave him alone and frustrated. Rather it might have been expected that he would have effected a total libidinal withdrawal, and would have destroyed any mental conception of the analyst. The pulling back of his thought as described above did show that this withdrawal and distinction was operating, but nevertheless the fact that the thought did occur suggests that, with the prospect of a lengthy separation, there is an intensification, a hyper-cathexis of the libidinal attachment to the separating object, perhaps in an attempt to reach him before the break and assuage the separation. In this way, the ambivalence of the relationship is demonstrated in action, and the fact that the thought had occurred in the analyst's absence between sessions and that the content of the thought was in the past tense adds to this. Psychical quality, meaning, and significance had emerged in the context of this ambivalent experience in this object relationship of patient and analyst, both internally and externally.

Bion (1962) in his paper on 'A theory of thinking' added further concepts to Freud's theories, and I shall briefly consider them as they are relevant for our theme. He wrote:

> It is convenient to regard thinking as dependent on the successful outcome of two main mental developments. The first is the development of thoughts. They require an apparatus to cope with them. The second development, therefore, is of this apparatus that I shall provisionally call thinking. I repeat – thinking has to be called into existence to cope with thoughts. It will be noted that this differs from any theory of thought as a product of thinking, in that thinking is a development forced on the psyche by the pressure of thoughts and not the other way round.
>
> (1962: 306)

He classified 'thoughts' into preconceptions, conceptions or thoughts, and concepts. The preconception corresponds to the infant's inborn disposition to the expectation of a breast; if this preconception is brought into contact with the realization of a satisfying breast, the mental outcome is a conception. If, however, this preconception is brought into contact with the realization that no-breast, an absent breast, is available for satisfaction, the mental outcome will depend on the capacity for tolerance of the frustration inherent in this no-breast experience. If the capacity for tolerance of frustration is sufficient, and this is presumably based on previous experiences of satisfaction, the experience of the no-breast inside becomes a thought, and an apparatus for thinking it develops. If, however, this capacity for tolerance is insufficient, then processes of modification or evasion become necessary.

He further conceptualized ideas of alpha-function and beta-elements. The essential feature of alpha-function is the process of generating meaning out of sensory data, and this is linked with the capacity to tolerate frustration of the sensations of the no-breast experience in the development of thoughts. If this capacity for tolerance is inadequate, alpha-functioning fails with the result that particles of undigested sensory data, or beta-elements as he called them, accumulate in the psyche and are dealt with by evacuation, a type of evasion. According to this theory, consciousness, being the sense-organ for the perception of psychical quality, is dependent on alpha-functioning and, if this is absent or deficient, then consciousness, meaning, and significance will be missing as described above. Furthermore, the development of the capacity for alpha-functioning depends on the capacity of the mother (breast) to contain the infant's projective identifications of nameless dreads, presumably constituted by beta-elements, and use her own alpha-functioning on them by behaving in a manner which converts the nameless dreads into tolerable anxieties that the infant can then re-introject. In this way, the mother enables the infant to develop its own capacity for alpha-functioning both directly and by identification with the mother.

If we apply these models of Bion's to the patient, we would say that alpha-functioning had not been operating in him until the event that the patient described as his first conscious thought. This thought was the result of (1) the mating of the preconception of the analyst, the breast, with the realization of the experience of satisfactory symbolic feeding to form a conception, and (2) the mating of this preconception with the realization of the no-breast experience, the analyst's impending holiday separation. The thought itself was of the analyst's presence – 'He was talking to me' – yet the timing of this thought, just before the break, clearly indicates the analyst's absence. The consciousness of the patient would also fit the model as described, as the beta-elements type of psychic functioning would have been made tolerable and acceptable to the patient by the reliability and interpreting ability of the analyst, his alpha-functioning, which was re-introjected and identified with by the patient.

Following the Christmas break, the patient had several episodes of these conscious thoughts. He had often told me during the course of his analysis that he had no mind, nothing to think with. Then just before the next Easter break, he said that I was building a mouth for him bit by bit and that this was his mind that he could think with. I asked him how he thought I was doing this building and he replied that it was because I had been satisfying him by feeding him (symbolically) and also frustrating him, and both of them were necessary. This extraordinary insightful statement sounds as though it had come straight from Freud or Bion but I knew that he was honest in never claiming the ideas of others as his own. Let us examine the theoretical implications of this.

First, the notion of a mind developing from both satisfaction and frustration is common to both Freud and Bion, but the notion of an apparatus for thinking being developed to cope with thoughts is specifically Bion's. These clinical observations lend support to his theory of thinking. I am, however, basing this on the assumption that when Bion talks of 'thinking' as an apparatus, this is equivalent to a mind, which is also an apparatus for thinking with.

Second, he had again given me this observation before a break in treatment, and again the context of the relationship between analyst and patient is one where the analyst is the active mouth-builder and the patient, the passive recipient. It seems that, again, the no-breast (absence) situation is essential for the mouth-mind building and in this situation of the no-breast, the position of the patient is essentially passive – or should it rather be termed receptive? The absence, actively imposed by the analyst-partner of the dyad, has to be endured and tolerated by the patient-partner. Yet this passive (receptive?) process is necessary for the development of an active mouth-mind, one for taking things in or spitting them out, as suggested by Freud (1925) in his paper on 'Negation', the forerunner of intellectual judgement, reality-testing, and taste.

Third, we should take note of the paradox that, although the mouth-mind is the organ for taking in and tasting meaning and awareness of thoughts, the very bricks of which it is built are such thoughts; this is the idea proposed by Bion.

Some months later, although this time it was not related to a treatment break, he told me that he was feeling whole and empty instead of being a nothing-in-bits. He was now developing a new higher conception of himself, what Bion described as a 'concept' or 'fixed conceptions or thoughts', that of self, even though it was an empty self. This would indicate that in order to have a concept or sense of identity, it is necessary to have a mind to develop and contain such a concept.

To summarize, I have described three levels of the experiencing of thinking:

1 thinking which is not felt to be conscious, nor yet is it strictly unconscious, and possessing no quality, meaning, or significance to the thinker;
2 thinking which is felt to be conscious, and possessing quality, meaning, and significance, but as yet consisting only of isolated thoughts;
3 thinking, as in (2), but now connected with possessing a mind that gives continuity to thoughts and possibilities of increased complexities in the conceptualization of thoughts.

The changes from one level to the next have occurred in the context of a satisfactory gratifying–frustrating relationship in the (symbolic) oral phase between analyst and patient. The experiences described lend some support to Bion's theory of thinking.

Note

1 First version published in the *International Journal of Psycho-Analysis*, 1968, 49: 709–11.

PART TWO

Technique

Issues and problems in
effecting psychic change

6

Types of transference interpretation: an object–relations view[1]

I want to discuss the various types of transference interpretation that have been described in the literature and how one sees them from the object–relations point of view. In order to do this, we need to clarify what we mean by the terms used in the title of the chapter. What do we understand by the terms 'object relations', 'transference', and 'interpretation'? I will attempt this clarification, but in order to keep it in bounds will be rather dogmatic by saying what I consider to be the meaning of these terms, which will help me better to develop my thesis.

Let us first take the term 'object relations'. This is usually used with the term 'theory' in order to distinguish it from instinct theory, and these terms distinguish formulations which are concerned with the individual's relations with his objects from those concerned with the individual's instinctual or drive developments. To quote Charles Rycroft (1968) on this distinction:

> Formally the distinction is a false one, since instincts are directed towards objects and objects can only be of significance if the individual has some drive to relate to them. In practice, however, it is a real one, viz. between theories which assume that the individual acquires the capacity to relate to objects at some stage of development and those which assume he is born related to an object (the mother); between those which assume that adaptation is a reluctantly learned process and those which assume that the infant is born adapted; between those which assume that the value of objects lies in their capacity to give instinctual pleasure and those which assume that the value of pleasure lies in its capacity to enrich relationships.
>
> (1968: 74)

I assume that although it is clear that the individual does go through intense instinctual developments and vicissitudes from birth that are essential for growth, there is equally a basic relationship with the mother from birth and almost certainly before birth, which rapidly extends to the father and others. These basic relationships and the personal qualities and attributes of the mother and other objects play a crucial part in the development and growth of the individual and of his internal psychic world throughout his life. This holds true for all relationships throughout life and it is this view I am adopting here, since it includes the person of the analyst.

If we now turn to the term 'transference', we are involved in a complex area since it is a term that has been used in many different ways; the excellent book by Sandler *et al.* (1973) gives a good account of the term's vicissitudes. I shall use their statement of the concept:

> We concluded that a useful statement of the transference concept would be to regard it as: 'a specific illusion which develops in regard to the other person, one which, unbeknown to the subject, represents, in some of its features, a repetition of a relationship towards an important figure in the person's past. It should be emphasized that this is felt by the subject, not as a repetition of the past, but as strictly appropriate to the present and to the particular person involved ... transference need not be restricted to the illusory apperception of another person but can be taken to include the unconscious (and often subtle) attempts to manipulate or to provoke situations with others which are a concealed repetition of earlier experiences and relationships'.
>
> (1973: 49)

I would add that these unconscious, or sometimes not so unconscious, manipulations are directed towards making the analyst behave in a way that would justify the patient in concluding that his apperception of the analyst was not illusory but real.

The last term is 'interpretation' and again I will turn to Sandler *et al.* for their account of its usage. To paraphrase from their summing-up (p.110), the term is used to mean the analyst's inferences and conclusions regarding the unconscious meaning and significance of the patient's communications and behaviour, and their communication to the patient. From these uses of the various terms, it is evident that a transference interpretation will involve two aspects of the patient–analyst relationship; one of the immediacy of that relationship, often called the here-and-now, and the other derived from the relationships of the past, called the there-and-then. The major part of the analytic work is devoted to the elucidation of these two aspects – that is, to transference analysis – but I want to make it clear that although I am dealing here only with transference interpretations, I regard the elucidation and helping the patient understand his extra-transference problems and relationships as an essential part of a psychoanalysis. Not to do so, in my opinion, is to minimize and devalue the patient's experiences and relationships with everyone except the analyst which will in itself distort the patient–analyst relationship in many ways. I am not a believer in the school of analysts that considers that only transference interpretations can bring about change – that is, are mutative, to use the terminology of Strachey (1934). We will examine these questions further when we come to discuss interpretations and psychic change in a later chapter.

One of the problems with which we are faced is to decide on the use to which we are going to put our interpretations. Is the function of transference interpretations to enable the past of the patient to be reconstructed, to be a sort of royal road understood by transference interpretations as it once was by dream interpretation? Or is it a way of exploring the external and internal object relationships in the here-and-now of the sessions and from this gradually to differentiate 'the specific illusion' of Sandler *et al.* from the actual reality and hence relating it to the past? Another way of putting the question is to ask whether transference manifestations only develop during the course of the analysis or whether they are present from the very beginning or even before the patient actually sees the analyst. My view is that the specific illusion is there from the beginning and earlier and it becomes more obvious as the analysis goes on, particularly because of the actual behaviour of the analyst in the analytic setting. These specific illusions constitute a most important aspect of the internal object relationships of the patient and the unconscious phantasy life that they represent. To quote Paula Heimann (1956):

> In spite of general agreement amongst analysts that the transference is the battleground, in other words that the dynamic changes in the patient's ego depend on the working through of his emotional conflicts as they centre upon the analyst, there are great differences in psycho-analytic technique as practised. These have often been defined in terms of the timing of transference interpretations, of interpretations of the negative versus the positive transference, or deep versus superficial interpretations, or the number of interpre-tations altogether. In the past – perhaps not only in the past – the analyst's efficiency was measured by the amount of his silence. These definitions, important though they are, do not go to the core of the matter. The essential causes of the differences in psycho-analytic

technique are in my view related to the analyst's appreciation of the role played by unconscious phantasy in mental life and in the transference.

(Heimann 1956: 305)

She goes on later, to state:

On this view, unconscious phantasy, the cause of the transference, is not something that occasionally irrupts into the patient's relation with the analyst and then interferes with his reason and cooperation. It is the fertile matrix from which his actual motives spring and which determine his apparently rational behaviour, his reasoned presentation of ideas and co-operative acceptance of the analyst's interpretations no less than his silence, or negativism, or openly defiant resistance.

(1956: 306)

She sees unconscious phantasy as underlying all mental life which includes all the specific illusions of the transference.

Betty Joseph (1985) in her paper on 'Transference: the total situation', stresses the idea of

transference as a framework, in which something is always going on, where there is always movement and activity. ... Much of an understanding of the transference comes through our understanding of how our patients act on us to feel things for many varied reasons; how they try to draw us into their defensive systems; how they unconsciously act out with us in the transference, trying to get us to act out with them; how they convey aspects of their inner world built up from infancy – elaborated in childhood and adulthood, experiences often beyond the use of words, which we can often only capture through the feelings aroused in us, through our counter-transference, used in the broad sense of the word.

(Joseph 1985: 447)

As an aside, we can recognize in this description the activities that I have described as characteristic of the hypnotic state – the drawing of the hypnotist into their defensive system, the acting-out with the hypnotist in the hypnotic transference relationship, colluding with him in the acting-out of the omnipotent phantasies of the inner world, and the analytic understanding of the relationship through the counter-transference. As has been said many times, transference is ubiquitous.

Pearl King has an interesting view on the handling of transference interpretations. In her paper (1971) she says:

It seems to me that (there are) two main theoretical approaches among psychoanalysts to the canalizing and utilization of transference phenomena within the therapeutic relationship, both of which stem from Freud's work, and these have led to the development of different approaches to the interpretation and use of transference phenomena. The first is that in order to enable a transference neurosis to develop and the illness to be experienced in relation to the analyst (and therefore become accessible to treatment) transference interpretations should not be made in the early stages of treatment, lest they bias or inhibit the growth of the transference neurosis, rendering the neurosis of the patient less accessible to treatment. The second approach arises from the idea that an understanding of the transference is the 'royal road to the unconscious' so that the quicker you can evoke the transference of early pathogenic material into the analytic relationship and towards the person of the analyst, the sooner you will have access to unconscious processes in the patient and be in a position to analyse his unconscious anxieties and conflicts.

A hypothesis that I have tentatively formulated is that the first approach can result in quicker access to neurotic areas of the patient's personality and the alleviation or cure of his neurosis, but it may leave relatively untouched those areas of the personality not directly involved in the presenting neurosis. The second approach, however, is what Wilhelm Reich called a 'character analysis', where the personality of the patient, well and ill, becomes involved in the analytic process and therefore in the process of cure.

(King 1971: 5)

It has often been commented on that the type of patient who comes to analysis has changed; they are not usually patients who have a specific neurosis but rather the vaguer complaints of discontents with themselves or with living, and these patients require a character analysis for the exploration of their total external and internal psychic life. This makes the second approach the more necessary one for the present-day analyst.

To illustrate this approach, I will give case material from the early months of a supervised analysis. The patient is an unhappy woman in an unhappy *ménage*; she has had some marital therapy and then been recommended together with her husband for individual analysis. It is a Thursday session; she lies on the couch and says that something is bothering her and she wants to mention it before the analyst does.

She hasn't yet returned her financial form (this is a clinic form regularly filled in by patients to ascertain their current financial position). She imagines that the analyst won't understand the terrible difficulty she has been having in trying to fill it in. She thinks he will just expect her to get on with it.

The analyst interprets that he thinks she sees in him an attitude of hers towards these difficulties, where she expects herself just to get on with it and not understand why it is so difficult.

She agrees with this and goes on to say that she doesn't think she really wants to give the analyst the form. She expects that she doesn't really want to give him any money. She says that it's funny that she should think of him as not understanding because most of the time when she thinks about him, she feels he is sympathetic. But she thinks that it's just that she can't feel that when she's actually here. Now that she thinks about it, she realizes that whenever people try to help her, she just spoils it – she just can't accept anything good. Her mother has been trying to be nice to her recently, but she (the patient) just mucks it up. Even in the coffee-break she has at work when she treats herself to a biscuit, it always seems to crumble up and she's left covered in crumbs.

This reminds her of a dream she had last night. In the dream, she gives her boss a biscuit. The boss starts eating it but the biscuit turns into a swarm of bees in her mouth – or maybe in her ear, because she complains she can't hear for the buzzing. The patient feels very guilty, so tries to make a placatory joke to her boss, but it doesn't come off.

The patient then goes silent and the analyst asks her what the joke was. She says that the joke was that she said the boss has gone all 'countrified' but that seems wrong, so she says 'ruralified', but that's wrong too, so she tries 'pastoralized', but even that's wrong. Then having told the joke, the patient is again silent.

The analyst asks her for her associations to the dream. She says that a biscuit is something sweet and good. She likes bees as opposed to wasps because they provide honey, but she realizes that they do sting. She is then again silent.

The analyst interprets that the dream seems to show that, indeed, she doesn't want to give him something good, but instead something that will attack him and stop him from hearing and understanding, since in previous sessions she had often spoken of confusing him. He thinks, however, that this also works the other way round, where what she sees as his good sympathy can become something bad that she fears will attack her from inside her.

She nods in response to this but remains silent. The analyst asks her about the words in the joke. She replies that to be 'ruralified' – well, her boss is supposed to be an expert on rural and urban environments and lectures on this. She is again silent. The analyst asks about the other words. She replies that she doesn't know about them. She likes to play with words when she talks to people and it sometimes makes her feel on top of people.

The analyst interprets that he thinks she's playing with words with him here, where 'countrified' means turned into a cunt, and 'pastoral-ized' is like pasteurized, which is milk made sterile. It all seems to involve a denigrated picture of a feeding mother who is being laughed at; this happens here when she feels he's sympathetic and trying to give her something good and she then denigrates him in her mind and feels on top of him; that he is supposed to be an expert but that really he's not.

The patient squirms on the couch, says nothing, and the session ends.

Whenever clinical material is presented, all analysts will have their own views on how they would have interpreted the material and how they might have chosen other themes to focus on; perhaps, say, the way the patient by her silences was putting the analyst too often into the position of asking for clarification or elaboration and so into his being a potential persecutor; or perhaps some might have included the extra-transference boss–patient relationship; or perhaps the patient's own bossiness. The interpretations offered were all transference interpretations in that they were all concerned with the possible meanings of the patient's utterances in terms of the analytic relationship in the here-and-now. The first interpretation concerned the projection onto the analyst of the patient's own superego feelings of expectations of performance, and this the patient accepted and then recognized her problem in not being able to experience the analyst as a sympathetic person in the immediacy of the here-and-now. The second interpre-tation concerned her withholding and attacking behaviour towards the analyst and her fears of his retaliation. The third interpretation linked with the second, added the analyst's imaginative use of his own phantasies on the word play, and, of great importance, introduced the notion of the denigrated feeding mother, a clear linking of the present with the past, forming a near-complete transference interpretation. It could be said that the overall themes of the sessions from the interpretations are the patient's needs to do things perfectly and without help in order manically to repair the damage done by her attacks on helping objects, including the primary object, and so avert her fears of the object's retaliation.

However, so far, the patient has given no confirmation or denial of the correctness of the analyst's interpretations apart from the squirm on the couch and the meaning of this movement is ambiguous, and so we

73

must turn to the next session to see if this is helpful in this respect. She lies on the couch and pours out a deluge of material in an excited atmosphere. She says that a couple of interesting things have happened since yesterday's session. She left feeling excited, she got to the Underground, took the escalator down, but ended up on a platform for trains going in the wrong direction. She feels pleased that her unconscious seems to be working and that important issues are forcing their way into her dreams. She's been thinking about her mother; she knows she wasn't breast-fed as she wasn't getting enough, and she doesn't think her mother persevered. She was also thinking about similarities between her mother and her boss. She used to idealize her boss just like her mother, but she doesn't do that now. At her coffee-break today, she had a biscuit to eat but she didn't feel she needed it – she felt she had some sort of internal sustenance.

I shall not give the rest of the session, but it is clear that the interpretations her analyst had made were probably on the right lines since they had excited her intellectually – and perhaps sexually from their sexual content, hence the squirm; the interpretation had enabled her to give information about her early relationships with her mother, and had enabled her to link that with her relationship to her boss. She had also allowed the interpretive food given by the analyst to remain good, as internal sustenance. Negative aspects are also indicated in her comments about getting on the wrong platform and this was taken up by the analyst later in the session.

The type of transference interpretation given in this material was addressed to a conflict which was present in the patient–analyst relationship, in this instance between the patient's hostile drives and the anxiety of the analyst's expected retaliation. Interpretations concerning a conflict with persecutory or depressive anxieties in this dependency relationship are basic to any analysis and may be on any level of ego or drive organization. They could be considered as interpretations of conflict in an anaclitic type of object relationship. These situations may be more complex as more than one conflict may simultaneously be present, and this may lead to a virtual paralysis of analytic activity unless this is understood and made clear by the analyst.

To give an example; a borderline schizophrenic patient had from the beginning of her analysis experienced great difficulty in being able to speak first in sessions. Over a few years, a lot of work was done on this problem with some improvement, but then it got much worse again and eventually it culminated in complete silence. Throughout one session I allowed the silence to go on and said nothing myself, particularly as I didn't understand why she had become so silent. Throughout the following session the silence continued and I found myself becoming increasingly angry with her and I wanted to throw her out since she seemed to be negating all my analytic work. Towards the end of the session she said that if the hurt that she had always had inside her came out, she would have to kill herself. She then wondered if I would stop the analysis. This was the end of the session and I said nothing. I then thought about my intense counter-transference feeling and wondered if she thought I would throw her out if she did speak and show me her hurt. The next session started in silence but after a few minutes, I interpreted by wondering if she was afraid I would reject her in the way her parents often had when she did show them her intense feelings, but that she was equally afraid I would reject her like her parents by her being so demanding that I talked to her instead of her talking to me. In this way she felt trapped and able to say nothing. She replied that that was absolutely right and after this, the situation improved and no further problems of this kind were encountered. She had recognized the two conflicts involved in the paralysis of silence and had also recognized that her phantasized retaliations were most unlikely to come true – in view of her experiences of my real and actual behaviour towards her as an analyst throughout the analysis. This was truly a mutative interpretation.

The other important type of transference interpretation is not one of an anxiety-ridden conflict of an anaclitic type, but is concerned with the awareness by the analyst of the narcissistic sensibilities and vulnerabilities of the patient and of the patient's great potential for experiencing feelings of shame and humiliation in the analytic relationship in any and every vicissitude of this experience. In order to be able to formulate such interpretations, we must have an empathic and intuitive appreciation of the feelings of the patient in his responses to the various aspects of the analytic situation, and within this situation, the most important appreciation of ourselves as we really are. We have to recognize our customary ways of behaving and speaking, of the form of words that we customarily use, to the tone of our voices, to our weaknesses and partialities. Only then can we really recognize the patient's responses to us as real objects in order to be able to help them eventually to make the distinction from phantasized objects. This particular type of interpretation, together with the analyst's awareness of his failures to be sufficiently sensitive to his patients, is one that Kohut (1971) has written on extensively, but he has done this at the expense of interpreting the patient's conflictual anxieties. He believes that only this type of interpretation is truly empathic and reconstructive, yet this does not accord with clinical experience. The example of the use of my counter-transference to understand the dilemma of my patient with her simultaneous conflicting anxieties, in my opinion,

needs every bit as much of my empathy and intuition as any understanding of her narcissistic vulnerabilities, which were certainly much
in evidence in that patient.

An example of this type of interpretation comes from the analysis of
a man who came to me feeling suicidal since he felt he had changed
into a woman who had just left him. He is, in fact, psychotic. This is
from a session after some years of analysis. He told me that he felt he
was all swollen up as he had been as a child and this was to make
himself bigger than me. He then said he felt he'd had too rich a diet. I
interpreted that my helpful and correct statements which he tried to
use to analyse himself were the too rich diet and that they made him
feel small as he couldn't produce such food himself; he then made
himself swollen with my interpretations to escape the feelings of
smallness, humiliation, and envy. He then said that he felt himself
resisting that statement. I replied that he would do that, as it was
another piece of the rich diet. He remained silent and then said that I
was quite right and that he felt terribly mean, like a bloody cannibal. I
replied that if he ate me, all the source of the richness would be inside
him and he would avoid feeling mean and small. He replied, yes, he
could also avoid seeing himself as he really is, mean, grudging, and
resentful. He started savagely to bite his finger-nails. I said that it
reminded me of the phrase about the dog biting the hand that feeds it.
He said that he didn't like that and that even if it was true, he felt as
though I were telling him off and punishing him. He saw himself as a
donkey with me as his master with a carrot and stick. I said that, like
the donkey, he didn't want any movement forward in his analysis. He
agreed very much with this but didn't like it as he said I was making
him feel useless.

In this example, the patient feels as though he were a child with a
mother who, by possessing all the resources of richness, persecuted him
in his envy of her in rivalling or surpassing her or even doing anything
for her in possible reparation. This is an anxiety-conflictual aspect of
the anaclitic relationship, but the narcissistic vulnerability concerns his
feelings of being small and useless in relation to this idealized maternal
figure and to recognizing the powerful feelings in this respect that my
interpretations arouse in him. I also have to wonder if I had been
telling him off since, in his sensibility, my words about the dog biting
the hand that feeds it may well have been experienced as a reprimand
and punishment. Furthermore, he shows, in his donkey-stubbornness,
one type of retaliation open to him in these circumstances, but in the
next session we see a different type of attack and a switch-round in the
narcissistic configuration.

76

He told me in a triumphant voice that nothing happened yesterday. Today he wanted to be the star and get all the praise and applause from me for the way he could destroy everything I had said and make nothing of it. He thought I must admire his cleverness at this, and that this was what he could do with his cleverness to avoid admiring the clever things I could say, which he couldn't. He said he couldn't stand the reality of the limitation of his intelligence as it tied him down. I shall not give the rest of the session but it is clear that he has reversed everything and now feels triumphant since the analyst is now the helpless child admiring and envying the patient's grandiose richness and cleverness that is used in the perverse service of the destruction of the analyst's idealized cleverness. Here the analyst is made to experience that which the patient–child had experienced in fact or phantasy in the past in relation to a parent figure, and the important thing was for me to understand it as just such a communication, that is, for me to understand what it was like for me to feel today as he did yesterday, and not simply to understand it as an envious and retaliatory attack on the idealized maternal figure of the analyst.

If we pursue the theme of empathy with the patient, we need to note that we are talking of a real object relationship with the patient since we are consciously and unconsciously putting ourselves in the patient's shoes in order to understand what he is feeling and thinking. However, we know that at times something inside us interferes with our empathic capacities and we may express ourselves in such a way or in such a tone of voice that it leads to resistance and hold-up rather than progress in the analysis. Usually the interfering something is our counter-transference, and it is often very necessary for this failure of our empathy to be recognized by us and acknowledged before further progress can be made in the area in which the failure occurred. I will give an example of this.

A borderline hysterical patient, after about two years of analysis, told me during a session that she hadn't said any more to me about her lesbian activities since the very early days of the analysis. She said that the reason for this was that when she had mentioned them to me, I had asked her about what actually happened in these activities and she had felt that I was just a prurient male trying to get some perverse sexual excitement out of lesbian activities and so had determined not to tell me any more. I couldn't remember what I had or might have said, so I told her this and asked her to tell me what she thought I had said. She told me and I thought about it, and then replied that if that was what I had said, it had not been a particularly sensitive way of putting it. She was quietly satisfied with what I said and she then told me that when

77

she was about ten years of age, her mother had come into her bedroom one night and got into bed with her. The patient was not yet asleep but she felt afraid and didn't move or speak. Her mother then started to caress the patient's genitals. This continued for a time and then her mother got out of bed and left the room and went back to her own bedroom. The patient had felt frightened and incensed by this behaviour of her mother and described it as an intrusion into her privacy. My failure of sensitivity towards this patient, which I believe had occurred because of my anger with her grossly acted-out intrusions into my privacy, had been experienced by her as my perverse intrusion into her privacy in much the same way as she had experienced with her mother. Whether the memory is a fact or a phantasy is not important for this chapter, but my acknowledgement of my failure of empathy allowed the patient to reveal important experiences from her past. It is not only that the making of interpretations directly linking the here-and-now with the there-and-then produces confirmatory or important new material, but so does the making of interpretations such as those just described above. A point to note is that I do not think it is appropriate or useful for the actual reasons for the analyst's lapse of empathy to be discussed with the patient since this would be to burden the patient with the analyst's problems, one of which may be exhibitionism, that do not properly belong in the patient's analysis.

At times the importance of the object-relationship aspects of the transference communications lies not in the content of the patient's associations but in the atmosphere or mood that is created in the session. This atmosphere can often be a pathway to the elucidation of earlier experiences that were connected with such atmospheres in the past. To give an example: in a patient's session, the thing that struck me most was not the content of the associations, but the feeling of emptiness in the air which I was also feeling. In the next session, the patient was talking of his sexual phantasies and the atmosphere was now one of excitement. I chose to interpret to the patient the change of mood and atmosphere in the sessions from that of emptiness on the previous day to excitement today, and I wondered whether the patient tended to escape from feelings of emptiness by filling it with sexual excitement. This led to him telling me of his compulsive masturbation when alone as a child. The interpretation of the mood or atmosphere of a session is an interpretation of the important non-verbal aspect of the transference relationship which can also lead us to the past.

A type of transference interpretation that I have yet to consider is one that is based on the response that the patient unconsciously makes to the analyst's interpretation. By this I mean that immediately after an interpretation, the patient's associations can often reflect in an unconsciously disguised fashion the patient's feelings and perceptions aroused by the interpretation. This is of great help to the analyst in checking his interpretations and in checking his own style of formulating or delivering interpretations and so enabling him to vary them if necessary according to the needs of the patient.

To give an example: I had been analysing a fairly placatory male patient for some years and he had now been talking of himself for some sessions as a 'vicious little bastard'. At one point I said to him that he felt afraid of bringing the vicious little bastard openly into the analysis. He responded by telling me a lengthy story about the family of a delinquent boy who often stole, and that in this family there was a father who, unlike the mother, was always getting at the boy like a prosecutor in a police court. I interpreted that he felt that I was like the prosecutor-father, getting at him for being a vicious little bastard and for keeping him out of the analysis. He agreed with this and told me that he had had a phantasy of my peeling his skull back and pecking at his brain about this. I shall give no more of the session, but the questions that I was then left to ask myself were whether I had behaved in too superego-like a fashion and persecuted him with the vicious-little-bastard phrase, or whether he really felt unconsciously guilty about his own behaviour and so experienced my statements as prosecuting-persecutory attacks. The answer to these questions would then determine whether or not I would modify my interpretive technique with him, and in this lies the importance of these clinical observations.

I now want to summarize the types of transference interpretation that I have described from the object-relations viewpoint:

1 interpretations aimed at understanding a drive-anxiety-defence conflict between patient and analyst in an anaclitic type of object relationship;
2 an extension of (1) in having two simultaneous conflicts of a similar and complementary nature;
3 interpretations aimed at understanding the sensibility and vulnerability of patient and analyst in a narcissistic type of object relationship;
4 an extension of (3) to include the interpretation of failure to achieve such understanding;
5 interpretations aimed at understanding the atmosphere or mood between patient and analyst which might be in either type of object relationship;

6 interpretations aimed at understanding the patient's unconscious response to the analyst's interpretations.

I will conclude by mentioning two other forms of transference interpretation. Since the importance of the here-and-now of the relationship has come into sharper focus, this, together with the increasing awareness of the mechanism of projective identification, has led some analysts into making statements such as 'You are putting your anger into me', or 'You are making me experience your confusion'. To quote Herbert Rosenfeld (1972):

> At the present time we occasionally find the converse situation where an analyst may relate all the material presented to him by the patient in a vague way to the transference such as 'You feel this about me now' or 'You are doing this to me' or they repeat the words of the patient parrot-like and relate them to the session. I think this stereotyped kind of interpretation, which is supposed to be an interpretation of the here-and-now situation, changes Strachey's valuable contribution of the mutative transference into something absurd.

These remarks are made as though they would be enlightening to the patient, but unless they can be supported by the clinical details of the patient's associations, they can either sound like magical thinking on the part of the analyst, or of his lack of comprehension and understanding, and are therefore better not made.

The second is not actually an interpretation but something that can be of equal value in its transference value and significance. I refer to the importance at times of not interpreting, but of remaining silent. Apart from the necessity of not over-interpreting and of giving the patient the necessary psychic space to develop his own thoughts and feelings in his own way, there are times, usually late in the analysis, when the patient is recovering contact with his lost original objects. This is an experience associated with mixed feelings, a bitter-sweet remembrance of sadness, regret, and love, free of paranoid hate and self-pity. These feelings of wholeness are extremely meaningful and moving for both patient and analyst and it is imperative for the analyst – in Balint's phrase (1968) 'the unobtrusive analyst' – to be there, to listen and to share, but above all, not to intrude with an interpretation, no matter how profound the analyst may think it to be. To give an example: late in his analysis, a patient was relaxed on the couch, rather tearful, slowly talking, almost as though to himself, that he had so often had bad feelings towards his parents, but really they had been very good to him and he felt so sorry for the ways he had been towards them. There was no sense of recrimination, or self-pity, or castigation of himself, but just a mood of awareness of what he had been like and the feeling of regret and sadness for it. I said nothing but simply felt with him in his sadness; most analysts would probably have behaved similarly.

Note

1 First version published in the *International Journal of Psycho-Analysis*, 1987, 68: 197–205.

7

Problems of management and communication[1]

The analysis of patients usually takes place with the analyst practising the classical technique as set out by Freud. The patient is expected to attend his sessions at the agreed times, to lie on the couch, and to free-associate as much as he feels capable. The analyst for his part will relax in his chair behind the patient, give his free-floating attention to the patient, and interpret as and when he feels it appropriate. Acting-out will be at a minimum and usually easily containable by interpretative means. However, with some patients this is not possible and other procedures, planned deviations called parameters, may need to be introduced in order to maintain and sustain the analysis. Parameters, a term introduced by K. Eissler (1953), is defined by Rycroft (1968), as a

> term borrowed from mathematics to describe those aspects of psychoanalytical technique which can (arguably) be modified to meet the needs of particular classes of patients. Frequency of attendance, length of sessions, degree of management of, and interference in, the patient's life, insistence or not on the use of the couch, are all parameters.

We should note the word 'arguably', since some analysts would maintain that the problems that arise in an analysis for which a parameter may be thought to be necessary, are really the result of incorrect or inadequate interpretative technique of the analyst. A proper understanding of the transference situation would result in the correct interpretation being given, and this would resolve the difficulties that had arisen. This, of course, is often the case, but the snag is that it is not always so; the problem may often lie with the patient's psychopathology and not in the analyst's deficient understanding. This is a complex issue and will be discussed later in the book.

Management can mean the taking over of, or interference in, the patient's life outside the analysis, and this is something that Winnicott, in particular, has written of in his various papers dealing with regression in patients suffering from borderline and psychotic states. However, management also means the way that the analyst conducts the analysis itself, not only in the ways in which he understands and interprets the patient's communications and needs, but also in the modes of communication that the analyst allows to the patient other than the strictly verbal. These too are complex issues and it is these that I want to discuss, and I would like first to illustrate the subject with certain aspects of the analysis of a borderline hysterical patient, one of whose symptoms were various forms of hallucination (Stewart 1977). The title of that paper was 'Problems of management', but it could equally well have been called 'Differing modes of communication in an analysis'.

The analysis

Elizabeth Zetzel in her paper on 'The so-called good hysteric' (1968), which mainly concerns women patients, made a useful classification of hysterical patients into four grades according to their psychopathology and prospects of analysability. My patient would, I think, fall somewhere between her third and fourth grades and I shall briefly delineate what these grades represent. To quote:

> Third, there are women with an underlying depressive character structure who frequently manifest hysterical symptomatology to a degree which disguises their deeper pathology. Fourth, there are women whose manifest hysterical symptomatology proves to be pseudo-oedipal and pseudo-genital. Such patients seldom meet the most important criteria for analysability.

She describes the fourth group as follows:

> However, while their symptoms may present a façade which looks genital, they prove in treatment to be incapable of recognizing a genuine triangular situation. For them, as for Oedipus himself, the parent of the same sex has not remained a real object in any meaningful way. Such patients all too readily express intense sexualized transference phantasies. They tend, however, to regard such phantasies as potential areas of realistic gratification. They are genuinely incapable of the meaningful distinction between external and internal reality which is a pre-requisite for the establishment of a therapeutic alliance and the emergence of an analysable transference neurosis.

My patient was not quite as ill as this and was, perhaps, also not a typical hysteric since severe depressions were one of her presenting symptoms. The discussion at the Paris Congress of the International Psychoanalytical Association (Laplanche 1974) showed the difficulties in defining the hysterical character, when compared, say, to the obsessional, and I do not wish to enter into that discussion here. I will, therefore, arbitrarily label her a borderline hysterical character.

She was referred to me by a colleague working in a hospital to whom a physician, on realizing that my patient might have some emotional disturbances to account for her recurrent fevers which had been present over a four-year period, had referred her. She was a young woman, looked rather wild and scruffy, wore torn jeans, and although she complained of depressions which had started with her first sexual experience ten years previously, did not have the typical depressive *facies*. During these depressions, she said she felt split in two, one part of herself wanting to be as bad as possible in her behaviour. This wanting to be bad, in fact, turned out to be almost a compulsion. She felt unloved and unwanted by everyone including her family and was unable to involve herself in any real way with anyone. She was working in a situation far below her capabilities. She was having an affair with a married man, was sexually subservient to him, was frigid and felt vaguely guilty about sex. There was little sense of identity or self-esteem. At the second session, she told me she wanted to be a man, that she felt that she was like a man and was a compulsive clitoral mastur-bator. This masturbation was experienced as if she were masturbating a penis that felt real, even though she knew that she did not possess one in reality, and she felt herself to be a man attacking a young child.

Her attitude towards her father, a successful professional man, was of scorn and contempt for his feebleness in the family circle, and she was frightened to some extent of her mother, who apparently held the family together, but who, in the patient's childhood, had shown uncontrollable tempers towards her children, doing them physical violence and then complaining to the children that they had hurt her by making her be violent towards them. The patient had an elder sister and a younger brother, neither of whom she really got on with. She had a delusional idea that her father was not her actual father but that she had someone called her 'real father', whom she had seen only once when she was five years old. This was by a canal near her home when she was out walking and he was described as a tall, dark man wearing an overcoat which, however, was buttoned up in the female fashion. Her actual father had been in the Forces since her birth and had only occasionally been home until his demobilization in 1946. At about this time she also thought she remembered her father's batman, her father

84

being an officer, exposing himself or doing something to her when he was staying in her parents' home.

Her only pleasurable experiences that she remembered from childhood were of her maternal grandmother who stayed with them during the war. She had been a kind, gentle, motherly woman, the only adult in the family whom the patient felt to be sane, and her departure at the end of the war, when her father returned, was a great loss to the patient. However, just to complicate matters, this grandmother used to see ghosts that no one else saw, but as these ghosts were benevolent by nature, they were not seen as frightening experiences.

The early stages of analysis were characterized by a careful and suspicious attitude towards me while she talked and expanded on her themes, but interspersed were runs of sessions when she would become mocking, provocative, denigrating towards me and the analysis, and anything I might say was twisted against me. These attacks of her being 'bad' ended by her saying she was sorry about them and hoped she had not hurt me. The attacks were based on her father's attitudes and behaviour towards her since childhood, as he had constantly mocked, undermined, or ignored anything constructive that she had tried to do. Her saying she was sorry was more placatory than genuine. Her mother's attacks were rather different and I shall now come to these.

After this initial gentle testing of me, the situation changed and I was faced with a difficult technical problem. For much of the time she wanted to be like a baby, to be with me or inside me, and hated the ends of sessions and weekend breaks. The problem arose from the fact that on occasions she would impulsively rush off the couch during a session and try to overpower me in a physical struggle, principally in order to find out, by feeling with her hand, whether I had an erection or not. At first I could stop her with verbal interpretations but these soon became useless and I had to decide what to do. This uselessness at times of verbal interpretations is a phenomenon well-recognized by all psychoanalysts who deal with very disturbed patients. I could have used threats by telling her that if she continued with this behaviour, I would have no alternative but to stop treatment, and possibly this threat might have worked. But I suspected that because of the very unrealistic nature of her desires, her behaviour was more compulsive than impulsive. Furthermore, I knew that she was the sort of person who, if prohibited from doing something, would immediately have to do it in order to see if the prohibitor meant what he said, and this would have meant the end of the analysis. I therefore adopted a different course, which was my first parameter, but which depended on a specific factor. This was that, physically, I was bigger and stronger than she, and hence I could physically prevent her from finding out what she wanted to

85

know. This meant physical struggles with the patient and I was concerned that this might then become a form of instinctual gratification for her with the danger of an addiction to an actual physical surrender to me becoming part of the analysis for her. I also had to examine my own counter-transference concerning close physical contact with a female patient but I decided that this was not the motivation of my decision. I wondered whether, if I were smaller, her acting out would not have occurred, but I doubt it because of the compulsive nature of her actions.

The result of doing this was very satisfactory for the course of the analysis. Over a period of months, instead of her becoming addicted to this behaviour, it slowly decreased in frequency as she discovered that I had control of the situation and not she, that I was being the sane, responsible person in the situation – perhaps like her grandmother – and she was gradually able to introject me as a sane control who did not punish or denigrate her or make her feel terribly guilty about her activities. It was then necessary, after these malignant acting-out activities, that the attempt be made to understand the meaning of these activities in terms both of the here-and-now of the analytic relationship and of her relationships with her past objects. This could be attempted in the 'good' interludes between the 'evil' ones. This is a vital technical procedure when dealing with regressions in analysis and cannot be too strongly emphasized. The important features of this aspect of the analysis were:

1 She intensely envied and wished to change and destroy my penis, particularly in its symbolic use as an understanding, penetrating analytic organ; her father had always thought of himself as intellectually superior to her. She wanted to sexualize our interaction in a concrete way in order to destroy my understanding of the situation, and in this destroy me as an analyst, together with her analysis.
2 I was regarded as a phallic mother or combined parent figure, and she was attempting to differentiate her confusion of the sexes by the presence or absence of the penis.
3 She felt herself to be the phallic mother, who was violent and uncontrollable as her own mother had been, whereas I was felt to be a helpless child-victim of these early experiences of violence.
4 I was experienced as the narcissistic extension of herself to do with me as she pleased, with my penis being her penis, and so actualizing concretely in phantasy, her own feelings of possessing a penis.
5 I was the male she wished to excite and triumph over sexually.

Gradually she became intensely dependent but ambivalent towards me, confused, empty, and depressed, and was now unable to work at her job. She dragged herself to her sessions and for the rest of the day did little but stay in her room. Her parents, who lived in a provincial town, were paying for her analytic fees and she existed on sickness and social security benefits.

She now started writing letters to me to keep in contact over weekends and holidays, and these were indicative of her state of mind. I quote from one letter:

> Dear Darling Dr Harold, I love you, I adore you, I worship you, and I cannot bear to be away from you. I hate you for arousing such feelings in me and not giving them any real outlet. . . . Take me back to your womb. I want to experience the world from inside you. I cannot exist separated from you. . . . Take off all your clothes. Show me that you have a penis. Show me that you can erect. I cannot bear it if you don't want me. . . . Go back to the devil you sprang from. Stop torturing me. Take your claws out of my body. Take your pick and shovel from my mind. You are plunging me into chaos. I want my hatred to worry you, to provoke in you the same degree of anxiety that I have to cope with. I hate your placid, self-sufficient manner. I think you are the most undesirable, unattractive, unsexy, uneverything object I have ever seen. I want to rip your clothes off. I want to whip you till the thickness of the lash is doubled by the particles of your flesh and blood tumbles from it like a waterfall.

Other letters were quite incoherent and unreadable. She was afraid of madness and of driving others mad. She was keeping contact with me for the whole week by means of letters as well as sessions and was fearful that this constant contact and dependence would drive me mad. But at least the contact was now verbal and no longer physical and I believe she was now experiencing me not only as the phallic mother but also as her phantasy 'real father'; you will recall the feminine aspect of him in the way the overcoat was buttoned up.

It was about a month before the Easter break of the third year of analysis that I became very concerned about her. After a Friday session, I developed the strong feeling that she might conceivably attempt to kill herself to escape from her torment and the coming weekend and Easter break, and I decided to act on my counter-transference feeling. I telephoned her to suggest that if she felt she could not cope with the weekend she could telephone me if she so wanted to. She thanked me, did not telephone and for the next week was more cheerful, presumably as a result of my display of concern about her. However, the outcome was the introduction into the analysis of a new form of communication that needed to be dealt with.

She came to the session with a packet containing some drawings. She placed the packet on my desk, left it unopened, and showed every sign of severe anxiety. She sat on the couch and told me she had done the drawings over the weekend and that she wanted me to see them. Yet at the same time she was quite terrified of their possible effect on me and did not want me to look at them then. Towards the end of the session she was fairly silent, rather hostile and anxious about me, saying she felt a looming black shape in the room. She was terrified about being in the room with the drawings which I had left still in their packet on my desk. She could not bear the anxiety and most unusually for her, left fifteen minutes early; usually she did not want to leave. At the next session, however, she felt more confident and was now prepared to look at the drawings and discuss them with me.

The drawings were of three distinct types. The first was of separate, discrete drawings done in charcoal, several to a sheet, the drawings varying from simple representations of objects to a more complex design of objects. The second type was a sheet covered completely with a highly organized complex design, particularly of faces, done in black and white with a felt pen. The outlines within the design were quite sharp. The third type was also a complex design covering the sheet but the outlines were less clear, there were no recognizable objects and, most significantly, they were in colour. It was these last drawings that were so very frightening to her, particularly one in black and red which she described as showing her obscenity and violence. It is perhaps to be expected that colour and indeterminate shapes would be the vehicle for the expression of a person's primitive aggressive sexual phantasies, rather than clear-cut black and white drawings.

Her initial terror of my response concerned what I might think of her having such phantasies and at the same time she must have felt that she had projected the blackness of the aggression in the form of the looming black shape into my room and so made it unsafe, but the reality of my normal response to her had allowed her to distinguish the reality of me and my room from her projections.

This sort of picture continued to be brought along to sessions and my problem was knowing how to deal with them. Because of the similarity of the styles, I had realized from the first that the patient had probably read Marion Milner's (1969) book *The Hands of the Living God*, and this she confirmed. This was probably another reason why the coloured pictures were so frightening to her, since they had not been copied from Milner's patient's style. But I also realized that I could never understand or interpret her drawings as Marion Milner did, as I do not possess her sort of artistic creativity, intuition, and insight for such use in the analytic situation. So I had to treat them like dreams, asking for her associations to the drawings and attempting to link them with her past and with the transference in the usual manner. But I also did not show an over-interest in them since I thought that if I did, my patient would most probably flood me with drawings. In the event she drew until the Easter break and after that almost dried up pictorially. It is of some interest that she later went to art classes for the first time in her life and has proved to have a good deal of talent, a good example of a removal of an inhibition.

The drawings were concerned with problems of separation together with her sexual and sadistic phantasies on almost every libidinal level or type of object relationship. Perhaps the most important aspects were her fear of the nature of her vagina, which was shown as having teeth or a beak, and fears of vaginal orgasm, as opposed to clitoral orgasm. The vaginal orgasm was seen as destructive not only to the erect penis of her partner, but also to the penis which she felt was hidden away inside her and only came out when she felt sexually excited and frustrated in her near-delusional phantasy. She had experienced puberty as castrating, as it meant that a real adult male penis had not developed at that time and hence if she now properly experienced her vagina, this would be the final blow to her desires to possess a penis of her own. The main threat to this blow was the analysis and the emergence of her femininity. She now had intercourse with a man, had no orgasm, but for the first time realized the terror of her vagina being the way it was in her drawings.

Her last picture was a complete coloured mess on the paper and it was done just before a holiday break. This came after one of her mocking, denigrating sessions and she described the picture as a smearing of shit all over my walls. This followed reading an account of the treatment of a woman called Mary Barnes. It could be shown to her that her behaviour had represented this shit – smearing over my insides to destroy everything inside me, including the potential babies I might return with after the break, and also to damage me for abandoning her and leaving her to hold her mad baby inside which she saw as empty and worthless. A dream also connected this with feelings of her abandonment by her mother when she, the patient, had been hospitalized for a fortnight when she was three years old and for being abandoned when she had started going to school.

We have now arrived at the time when her hallucinations began, in the third year of analysis, during the summer break. I received a letter from her during the holiday when she was motoring in Europe – although she was unable to work, she could still drive. I shall quote the relevant passages from it:

89

This holiday is proving disastrous. I have been attacked by a ghost, abandoned by the bloke I went with, and raped by a madman. I was staying in a Youth Hostel when I was assaulted in the night by an ancient Spanish roué, dressed in clothes from the Regency period, perhaps. I struggled with him for what seemed ages, finally fighting him off. Then I put my hand straight through him and realized he was a ghost. Up till then I had been convinced he was real. Then I was aware of his decaying body rotting away beside me on the bed, and I sat at the end of the bed frozen with horror for about an hour. After a very long time, it dawned on me that perhaps it wasn't a real ghost but a hallucination. I didn't know which alternative was the worst, but I began, semi-automatically to analyse my reasons for producing such a vicious ghost. Anger seemed to be predominant in me. I was angry with the fellow I went with because he's a lazy, insensitive, self-satisfied bastard and there was no real contact between us. But I think I pushed onto him my angry transference feelings, also my sexual feelings, to a lesser extent.

It seems to me that her analysis of the situation is essentially correct in relating the hallucination to her experience of me, although I do not think I am quite as bad as all that, but I think her feelings were of murder and fear of murder, rather than anger, as shown by her horror of the decaying, rotting body. This is one of the points made by Bion (1958) in his paper 'On hallucination', where he quotes Freud to the effect that the patient's state of mind and feeling is under the sway of the pleasure principle, and in that phase of development the patient's actions are not directed towards a change in the environment but are intended to unburden the psychic apparatus of accretions of stimuli. My patient seemed to be doing this as well as trying to change the environment in that she did fight with her hallucination.

I expect I could be phantasized as an ancient Spanish roué, and the fight she was having could also reflect her actual experiences of her physical struggles with me, but her mention of the Regency period clothes is very significant. She comes from one of the English towns that are graced by the Regency style and atmosphere and there seems little doubt that this ancient roué also contains the reference to her father and her childhood. This well fits in with Freud's view mentioned in 'Construction in analysis' (1937) that there is method in madness, and it is the fragments of historical truth which give the compulsive belief in delusions and hallucinations its strength, since it derives from infantile sources. I also think that this mixture of present and past experience that is contained within the hallucination is a good example of a compromise symptom.

Two further incidents occurred on this holiday which confirmed the feelings of anxiety concerning suicide that I had had, by her flirting with death in a near-suicidal way. She went swimming in the sea but so far out in a heavy current that she had to be saved by local fishermen while clinging to some rocks. After this she drove back about a thousand miles across Europe with the rubber on her tyres so worn that the canvas was exposed. These actions represent an extreme challenge to death and also help to confirm my method of dealing with her challenging acting-out in the early stages of the analysis.

On her return she had intense desires for intercourse with me and, when thwarted, masturbated continuously. She then saw another ghost in her bedroom and this was a little man three feet tall with fair hair and blue eyes who carried a rope and a bucket. She had a great fear on seeing it but then said to herself that it was a ghost and it disappeared. Apparently it resembled her younger brother who was born when she was eight years old. She then had more mocking, denigrating sessions and behaved badly to her parents while at their home. I was able to show her that the attacks on me followed the separations of the holiday and my refusal to have intercourse with her, and also displayed the envy of her mother for having the younger brother. The three-feet-high ghost probably represented the third year of her analysis and was her baby in the form of a hallucination. The attacks on her parents were to destroy their intercourse and happiness and also to destroy her own treatment, since they were paying for it, out of guilt for her attacks and also to show what a useless analyst I was. At the next session she told me she realized the correctness of this and then disclosed her phantasy of having two babies inside her, one a mocking, green, envious baby and the other, a pale, almost lifeless baby that she had to keep starved. This one was the sensitive, feminine baby that could easily be hurt. The compulsive, angry, envious penis phantasies came from the first baby and her problem was that the more loving she felt, the more she hated the separations from me and so this second baby had to be kept starved of love although she desperately desired it. This corresponds with Bion's views on hallucinations.

At the session after this she told me that she had seen her 'real father' again for the first time since childhood and he had said something to her but she didn't know what. She realized she had been hallucinating, but following this experience she felt that her mind had altered and somehow had come together for the better, and she now started to make herself a dress. This was the first breakthrough of her feminine self. This 'real father' was probably me representing some good split-off infantile aspect of her actual father for whom she had always longed.

At the next session she told me of having had a hallucination of a large penis on herself, then she became her mocking, biting, attacking self, but at the end of the session wanted to kiss me better. She then saw the film *The Devils* which is about the nuns of Loudon and later that evening had a persistent vision of her genitals rotting away. On putting her hand there, she felt a large hole where they had rotted away and was terrified. She then realized that this was another hallucination, a negative hallucination this time, and was then able to feel her genitals. She wanted to know if she was going mad and I said that for that moment she had been mad. She broke down and cried, but then linked her hallucination with the hysterical mad nun in the film who had licked the blood of her beloved priest's wounds after his torture, putting her tongue into them. I linked up her torturing treatment of me in the previous sessions with the priest's torture and of her intense desire to remove the source of her sexual desires by hallucinating away her genitals or to give herself the penis instead. She accepted this and told me that I tormented her with desire but did not gratify her and so she tortured me in return but was then afraid of driving me away. She was also tortured by humiliation at her failure to seduce me, but she then became afraid that she would hallucinate me away completely and that she would not be able to see or hear me and then she would be quite mad. This so bothered her that she gave my telephone number to her sister in case this might occur. She also broke down in tears at her art class. These events were important since, for the first time, she was really acknowledging to herself and to others that she was ill.

She now had a significant dream of my wife being pregnant and she herself feeling left out. Her associations were to a period of her childhood when her father had recently returned from the Forces; her parents had then quarrelled a lot and temporarily separated into different bedrooms, her father's being next to hers. She had then been shattered when her younger brother had been born when she was eight years old. This dream was soon followed by a pregnancy phantasy where she felt very heavy and wanted to urinate excessively. Apart from the transference aspects, she came out with the idea that her father had wanted to kill her when she was eight years old. This was the time when her brother was born and the conclusion must be that she had wanted to kill her father at this time. Thus her murderous feelings of jealousy and abandonment by her father at the birth of her brother, together with desires for his disappearance, came out more fully into the open. By now she was wearing the new dresses that she had made, used cosmetics and perfume and in every way was more feminine. After eighteen months off work, she was now able to return and, of equal importance, she was able to allow herself to regress much further during her sessions since she was developing the confidence that at the end of the session she would reintegrate and would not stay in a regressed chaotic state. She was developing a real sense of self.

By this time she had had several types of hallucinating experience and we began to recognize that there were various levels of this experience. The first was in recognizing that she could see things around her, but knew all the time that the experiences were not real and came from her imagination. The second was a state where she was not sure if the experiences were real or not; this made her feel afraid and so she switched her mind off in case they did become real.

The third state was where things came on her very suddenly out of the blue with the conviction of reality and it took some time before she was able to recognize that these experiences were not real. This state was usually preceded by feelings of anxiety, and she could not say why she should feel anxious. In my view the third state contains truly dynamic unconscious experience-phantasies coming from the id and the anxiety preceding their emergence is probably a subliminal awareness of them by the deeper layers of the ego. In a previous chapter, I have discussed hallucinations in terms of ego-splitting. Since they represent repressed instinctual and affective states, the anxiety on the ego's part is hardly surprising when the danger of their becoming conscious arises. The first state, when she is aware of their unreality from the start, must represent preconscious ego-phantasies, and the second state, a borderline area between the first and third states.

So far, the third state had always occurred outside the sessions and I pointed out that she was keeping these experiences in their immediacy away from me. The effect of this statement was to make her feel I was persecuting her by trying to drive her mad in the sessions by asking her to hallucinate. She felt I was not interested in her as a person but only as an object from which I could learn about mental functioning – a statement with some truth in it. She also felt that she could now triumph over me by keeping me frustrated in not producing these phenomena. Yet, at the same time she knew and acknowledged that I was right and that the chances were that she would not be driven mad by them. But I also knew that in showing this interest in her hallucinating states, it was quite on the cards that she would produce them for me in abundance in typical hysterical fashion. In the event, I do not think she did, but before getting on to them, another phenomenon turned up which was in fact rather similar to a proper hallucination.

While talking on the couch, she would suddenly shout out a word or phrase that could have had meaning in the context of the rest of what she was saying, yet by its nature seemed to come from another layer of the mind as an intrusion of a rather explosive nature. It often

93

contained a parapraxis that altered the sense of what she was meaning to say. For example, during the session when she felt I was trying to drive her mad by suggesting she bring her hallucinations into the consulting room, she felt confused by the knowledge that I was also the person who was trying to help her and had enabled her to return to work. She felt she loved me, wanted to put her arms around me, wanted me to put my penis inside her, and then shouted, 'Perhaps the penis is too exciting for you.' She then said that she had been going to say quietly, 'The penis is too exciting for me.' The problem here was to know (a) whether she was talking to herself and admonishing herself as though she were two people, like Lewis Carroll's Alice in Wonderland, or (b) whether she was telling me that I, the analyst, could not cope with the excitement that I might have in my penis and so was perhaps driving her mad by overstimulating her and so creating confusion, or (c) whether both were correct. Since she started the next session by telling me I was analysing myself, having just seen my new copy of Kohut's *Analysis of the Self*, and also telling me that I was writing notes to myself, on seeing a scrap of paper with writing on it on my desk, it seemed to her that the notion that I could not cope with the excitement in my penis was correct. But when she next said that the previous night she thought that I was inside her and that she was me, it seemed that the possibility of the penis being too exciting for her might also be correct and that she dealt with the exciting penis by incorporating and identifying with it. So in analysing her, I was also analysing myself. Furthermore, 'you' and 'me' could represent projected and introjected objects from the past. This may illustrate some of the problems involved in interpretation and understanding and the potential overdetermination of these statements.

I was seeing her in the early evenings and, being winter, it was dark outside and she now wanted to have only one light on in the consulting room so that it was rather dim and peaceful. She would go into a reverie-like state, like a child in a nursery with the dim light, and I had to remain very still in my chair, since any undue movement on my part would disturb her reverie and also make her feel, in a near-delusional way, that I was undoing my trousers or masturbating and this frightened her. She had the phantasy of being a small child sitting on my knee and of being bounced up and down on it by me, exciting her until she wet my trousers. She wanted to suck my penis, my breast, or her thumb and had an intense desire to masturbate. She then suddenly jerked round, felt that I was hitting her and shouting that she mustn't do that. This seemed to refer either to her wetting with excitement or to her desires to masturbate. At the next session she felt she was being driven mad by her desires to urinate and to masturbate and wanted to cut off my hands. She also had the compulsive phantasy that I had undone my trousers and was playing with my penis. She then jerked round, shouting, 'You shouldn't do things like that.' She then thought that she had meant to say, 'say things like that', instead of 'do things like that', which again contains the problem of who the 'you' is, but she went on quickly. She covered herself with her coat, which had been on the couch, and held her genitals, saying, 'I must masturbate.' She then felt horrified at this action of hers. I moved slightly in my chair and she screamed, 'I don't know what I'm so frightened of.' I did not know whether she was afraid of my punishing her for her action in holding her genitals; whether she was afraid she might have excited me sexually and that I might assault her sexually in some way, since there had been so many references during the analysis of a real or phantasied traumatic sexual assault on her as a child; or whether she was having the phantasy that she was me, or I her, and that she was secretly masturbating in phantasy and controlling me and that my punishment was towards this aspect of her masturbation rather than a straight-forward Oedipal punishment. It was even more complicated since I did not know whether the penis was father's or mother's, although I strongly suspected the latter since mother was felt to possess everything.

The next session was devoted to her playing a very complex game with various objects in my room, having them stand for various part-objects or aspects of mother, father, analyst, or herself. It was like watching a child playing with its toys. A most important object was my ashtray, which is a container on a tall column, kept by the side of the couch for the use of patients, and this stood for the phantasy penis. It emerged that her possession of this was essential to prevent the confusion in her mind of all the other parts moving around and splitting. She made a slip about her being the 'baby analyst', which I think referred to her feeling of not being the adult analyst, who has the penis with its penetrating and understanding qualities to bring things together, but only a baby amateur analyst; but I also think it referred to her feeling of having had to try to understand the confusing aspects of her family from an early age and to be the father, who was absent and later devalued.

This was followed at the next session by her telling me that the batman, her father's army valet, always used to wash his hands. She then placed her hand on her genitals and told me she could notice a strong smell of soap in the room. I could not smell anything myself, but she then bit her hand which, she screamed, was 'his soapy hand'. Here was the first hallucination, an olfactory one, during the session, and it was associated with a fairly obvious identification with this person, concerning the hand and the genitals and linked with a masturbatory action. I must confess that I could not clearly see the transference aspect unless this was an attempt to wash away the guilt she experienced from having tried to possess my analytic penis for herself only and using me as her batman. A great deal of the analysis concerned her desire to be a man, and for her to possess the penis represented a defence against internal chaos, depression, and emptiness. On one occasion when I collected her from the waiting room, she hallucinated that my trousers were undone and my penis was showing, but her associations were to the fact that she had seen my trousers in a different colour from what they were and that this colour corresponded to her mother's trousers. This led her on to realizing that she also experienced me as a mother who was false and phoney, untrustworthy and interested only in money and sex. I had always felt quite sure that one aspect of her emphasis on the penis and its possession was a defence against her vaginal desires and phantasies with the jealous rivalries and envies of her mother's vagina and womb at both Oedipal and pre-Oedipal levels, and as I previously mentioned, in the transference I was usually either a phallic mother or the phantasy 'real father' with his feminine overcoat, making it a bisexual transference figure. Yet at the same time, the hallucinations and verbal interruptions continued to suggest early traumatic assault by a man, not by her violent mother, and of her having witnessed parental intercourse. I had the classical difficulty of not knowing if I was dealing with actual traumatic experience or with unconscious phantasy. In one session she shouted, 'No, don't,' and then had the phantasy of a large man bending over her and she herself feeling little. She suddenly realized that she had used the same words to the little ghost who had resembled her brother but there was now a reversal of sizes, and this realization caused more mind-clearing.

There were other hallucinations but, most interestingly, she revealed a strange practice that she used in her bedroom. She would construct an artificial penis for herself with a stuffed rubber glove tied around her, and also make a female doll-like figure. She would then draw the curtains so that the room was very dim and would then have intercourse with the doll, she being a man and the doll a little girl. At times she would reverse the constructions and make a man, and she would be the little girl and the man-doll would have intercourse with her. This was an acting out of her masturbation phantasy. Perhaps the most important aspect of this is the negative one that the two figures were never equal, that is, man and woman, and this corresponded with her view that, in spite of everything she said, her mother was basically seen as having a worse deal out of life than her father and was always in the inferior position.

She was by now feeling greatly improved, was working hard at her job, cleaning and painting her flat, painting well at art classes and also doing some writing which she had always wanted to do. She had also found herself a proper boyfriend and he was an interesting choice. He was a large man who suffered from impotence and she treated him on behavioural therapy lines sexually and gave him the sexual potency he had lacked. It was as though she was creating a potent adult penis for herself and at the same time repairing the damage the penis had suffered for which she had felt guilty throughout her analysis. It was just before having intercourse with him on one occasion that she had what she described as a 'devastating hallucination'. It was not of a penis this time, but of a 'violent cunt', twisted and distorted like a Francis Bacon painting, and she now realized how terrified she was and had been of her mother and of her mother's violence which she had experienced as a child, together with the violence that she felt existing in herself and her genitals. The penis phantasy had long been a defence against this 'violent cunt' phantasy and she now in experience realized that I had been right in this assessment from the start. She is now capable of orgasm through vaginal intercourse, is married to this man and wanting children, knowing she will have her violence towards them under control.

Discussion

This analysis illustrates some of the problems encountered in the analysis of severely disturbed patients and, before looking further at these, we should see the different ways by which the patient has communicated with the analyst. The sequence of the emergence of these has been as follows:

1 By verbal-oral means, together with the unconscious projective identificatory mechanisms that give rise to some of the counter-transference feelings and ideation. This is the standard mode for all analyses.
2 By bodily physical contact.
3 By writing letters, both legible and illegible.
4 By drawings of various types.
5 By hallucinatory experiences, visual, olfactory, and tactile.
6 By other states associated with the lighting in the room and the game of analysis with small objects.

At this point, one of the many problems arises and this involves communication. It can be argued that the nature and forms of the communication in an analysis will depend on whether or not the analyst is prepared to accept them as such. This is a different issue from the one I raised previously concerning whether the emergence of these various forms of communication, which can also be called acting-out behaviours, is the result of the analyst's deficiency in understanding of the total situation, to use Betty Joseph's term. Even if we accept that these different modes of communication are a concomitant of the patient's psychopathology, does the analyst's tolerance and acceptance of them encourage further acting-out and encourage further modes of communication? Is this perhaps an example of a collusive relationship between the patient and me to avoid more painful issues in the transference relationship? To take an example, since I was unable to prevent the malignant physical acting-out of the patient in her attacks on me, was I colluding with the patient in acting in the way I did, and should I have perhaps sent her to another analyst who might have been able to deal with her in a more classical way without the patient acting-out in the way she did with me? This would have been a painful decision for me to accept, so was I avoiding it? To take another example: when the patient brought the analyst her drawings, should I have only interpreted the defensive aspect of this activity and not have examined their actual form and content with the patient on a mutual basis?

These questions are all part of an important issue in the theory and technique of the analytic situation. This issue can be stated as follows: are all communications, other than oral-verbal and the projective identificatory counter-transference concomitants, only defensive in their nature, or are they also important communications of unconscious experience which need to be made in that mode as well as being verbally understood in interpretative terms of the total situation? It should be noted that the issue is not that of understanding the emotional relationship of analyst and patient in interpretative verbal terms versus the emotional experience of other modes of communication; it is of the former versus the latter plus the understanding of the emotional relationship in interpretative verbal terms, but only after the emotional experience of the other mode has taken place. This, and related issues, will be further examined in the chapters on regression and on psychic change, but I do here want to answer the question about whether I should have sent the patient to another analyst. Masud Khan (1972), in writing on the analysis of a similar patient, described how she had already destroyed two psychotherapies and one psychoanalysis by her violent and destructive behaviour. He had noted that during her previous analysis with a female analyst, she had at one time been hospitalized, where she had been most helpful and compliant with the hospital staff, whereas her rages and demands had been reserved for her analyst. He managed the situation by setting strict limits to his tolerance of her behaviour; if she were too dreadful during a session, he would stop the session and tell her to return the next day, which after much protest, she did, and gradually her behaviour improved. It was the limit-setting, the parameter, and not simply the interpretative work that helped and contained both of these patients to stay in treatment.

I think it would be fair to say that the only parameter absolutely required in this analysis was the initial physical containing of the patient. Apart from this, the other modes of communication could have been so interpreted from their first appearance that the patient would have recognized that they were not really acceptable to the analyst, and the chances would be that this would have resulted in the oral-verbal communicative mode of classical analysis. Or perhaps only some of these other modes would have been truly accepted as such. Whether the analysis would then have produced a more or a less successful outcome than the one described here, I have no means of knowing. The problem of evaluating outcome in psychoanalysis is a sore and very difficult one, and the problem of comparing and evaluating differing techniques in analysis is even more so. In these circumstances, each analyst will have his own ideas on technique and outcome, based on his experiences of his own personal analysis and the analyses that he has conducted, and his reading of the literature; inevitably this will be based as much on mythology as on scientific validity.

My own view on these technical procedures is that, if presented with a non-verbal communication such as a letter or drawing, I would accept it, discuss the content, and also discuss the patient's need to communicate in this way. Usually this is sufficient for the patient to continue communicating in the classical way, but in some severe acting-out patients such as the one described, this would not work and I would then have to choose between acceptance or formal refusal of the communication. I would prefer to choose the former but this would always be accompanied by interpretations of the meaning, both defensive and communicative, of the patient's behaviour. We must not forget that non-verbal communication communicates something over and above the words that it can be translated into and this may be an essential communication. It is possible that this essential aspect may otherwise take years to be communicated orally-verbally, if at all. It is like trying to express a musical thought or feeling in words – it can't really be done. However, we must also recognize that one of the problems of non-verbal communication is that it can come to be used, not for essential communicating, but only for the gratification of the activity. This may then become a step in the development of a malignant regressive state rather than a benign one, and we shall examine this further in the chapter on regression.

One of the important factors in assessing the nature of these non-verbal communications is the counter-transference of the analyst. I am using the term in its widest sense to include both the analyst's empathic identificatory response and his reactive response to the projections of the patient. These counter-transference feelings will give important indications as to how the analyst should respond to the patient. It was, for example, particularly necessary for me to question whether my physical handling of her was in the interests of my sexual gratifications rather than the ego-containing needs of the patient. Similarly, the feelings of being manipulated or not by the patient in her non-verbal communication will determine the analyst's technical response. Whether the analyst's response is to the patient's ego-needs or to her id-wishes, to use Winnicott's terminology, can often only be decided by the analyst's counter-transference.

A word should be said, not on technique, but on an aspect of the psychopathology of these patients. I mentioned in the account of the analysis the patient's great desire to be a man. A most important motive for this desire was her unconscious belief that possession of the penis was a defence against terrible feelings of internal chaos, depression, and emptiness. This is also a feature of similar female patients that I have treated. One constructed an internal penis for herself by having the near-delusionary hallucination of urinating through her vagina via a hole between her bladder and vagina; this is akin to the male who has one urethra for both semen and urine, and this too was a defence against feelings of threatened chaos. The parental pattern of these patients was of a father who was disappointingly weak or absent, and of a mother often physically violent or disturbingly unpredictable. The infant's way of dealing with this was to try to be the father herself by internalizing the penis. This unconscious, or not-so-unconscious, phantasy of possessing the penis has to be understood and worked through at all levels, not simply in terms of penis envy, but of the pathological relationship with a disturbed mother and later, with a disturbed father.

Note

1 First version published in the *International Journal of Psycho-Analysis*, 1977, 58: 67–76.

8

An overview of therapeutic regression

The subject of regression, and particularly its use in therapy, has had a chequered career in the history of psychoanalysis, and partly because of this, the topic has been of interest to many therapists. Therapeutic regression has been present from the beginning, and even before the beginning, of psychoanalysis and in order to understand its vicissitudes, we should start by briefly recapitulating what we mean when we speak of regression.

Regression is regarded as the opposite of progression and in general refers to a reversion to an earlier state or mode of functioning. The term was first used by Freud in the last chapter of *The Interpretation of Dreams* (1900) to provide an explanation of the fact that dreams are hallucinatory phenomena and that this differentiates them from remembering. He assumed a normal progressive direction of processes in the mind, starting with the perception of a stimulus and going first towards thought and then to action, thus reducing the psychic version of the stimulus. If action is not possible, a regressive movement occurs which in normal waking life goes to memory-traces; regression beyond that point to the perceptual elements of experience gives rise to hallucination in the waking state or dreams in the sleeping state. In the third edition of this book in 1914, he later distinguished three types of regression, which he called the topographical, the temporal, and the formal. The topographical concerns the backward movements of mental processes as described above, and takes place in space; the temporal takes place in time and is from the present towards earlier experiences; the formal concerns behaviour observable clinically in which the more complex and advanced forms go back to simple ones.

Regression is also conceptualized as a mechanism of defence in which the subject seeks to avoid anxiety by returning to an earlier stage of libidinal and ego-development. This concept is linked with that of fixation-points towards which the regression occurs. Freud followed the English neurologist Hughlings Jackson, in his conceptualizing of

101

mental processes, in that earlier, simpler forms of functioning are superseded by later, more complex forms and that any type of inhibition or damage to the later forms will result in the reappearance of the earlier ones. Looked at in this way, regression can occur in terms of libidinal drive level, in terms of object relationships, in terms of the structural theory of the mental apparatus of id, ego, and superego, in terms of the positions from the depressive to the paranoid-schizoid. Lastly, we have the concept of therapeutic regression, where regression, particularly of the formal type, acts as an ally of therapeutic progress and is typically associated with the patient's dependence on the analyst. It is in this concept of regression that controversy lies and it is to this aspect that we now turn.

Earlier I mentioned that regression has been present from the earliest days of psychoanalysis and even before that, and, in this, I am referring to the original use of hypnosis as a therapeutic procedure. We should remind ourselves that it was a hysterical patient of Joseph Breuer, Anna O., who, by going into hypnotic trance-states and recovering lost memories that were associated with individual symptoms, gave her physician the gift of a new therapeutic procedure, the use of emotional abreaction of repressed traumatic experiences to remove symptoms. Breuer accepted the gift and proceeded to induce hypnotic trance-states himself in Anna O., to expedite the process. But, unfortunately for him, when faced with a hysterical miscarriage in his patient when he had decided to terminate treatment, he became so anxious about such consequences of this type of therapy that he could never again use these procedures. Fortunately for us, he had related his experiences to his young friend, Sigmund Freud, who, made of sterner mettle than Breuer, decided to pursue this technique for himself, and from this psychoanalysis was born. The point of interest in this for us is that hypnosis is a form of regression. The patient is induced by himself or the therapist into an altered state of consciousness of varying degrees, exhibits various types of behaviour, some being quite bizarre, in accordance with the suggestions of the hypnotist, and develops access to past memories and experiences which were previously inaccessible to the normal waking state.

Freud gradually gave up the use of hypnosis in his quest for the recovery of traumatic past experiences and instead developed the technique of free association, the key to psychoanalytic technique, which in turn led to changes in the aims of therapy. However, even though hypnosis itself was given up, a great deal of the actual therapeutic setting was retained in the analytic situation. The use of the couch, a quiet warm room not too brightly lit, frequency of sessions, an attentive therapist are all in fact aids to promoting regression in the patient. Free association itself in encouraging the patient to give up the vigilance and logic of ordinary secondary process thinking tends towards the establishing of more regressed, primary process, dream-like states. These then are the concomitants of the standard analytic situation – the patient lying on the couch, freely associating as well as he can, the analyst behind the patient listening to and being with the patient, occasionally commenting or offering an interpretation, and the sessions of a fixed frequency beginning and ending on time. However, with some patients this pattern is interrupted to a greater or lesser extent, and it is to these changes that we must now turn.

Breuer was the first therapist really to experience such a change. Instead of his patient going into a hypnotic state and verbalizing her experiences, she presented him with the shock of a hysterical mis-carriage, which he was able to treat by hypnotizing and quietening her and then departing as fast as possible. The sexuality of this asexual virgin proved too much for him. Freud, in his turn, having hypnotized a female patient, found that she threw her arms round him in great passion, whereupon he called for his maidservant to remove her. He recognized the sexuality but was not too disturbed by its manifestation. It is such behaviour that we would call acting-out or else describe as formal regression. The patient acts or repeats or regresses rather than remembers and recollects, and on the whole, it is found in hysterical female patients, particularly with male analysts. It is more often the case that the patient does not necessarily act herself but wants or requests or demands that the analyst should gratify her needs or wishes as the patient sees them. These requests or demands may seem innocent or not so innocent but the therapist is still faced with a situation with which he must deal.

How does he deal with such regressive behaviour in therapy? This, of course, will apply to all forms of analytic psychotherapy, since, although the instances given above occurred in hypnotherapy, they are in fact ubiquitous. Freud had no doubts on this score and his opinions must have been based on his own and his colleague's experiences with such patients. As far as he was concerned, therapy had to take place in an atmosphere of abstinence and privation as far as these issues were concerned and any attempt to do otherwise was fraught with the potentiality of dire consequences. He was well aware that improve-ments could occur if satisfaction of these requests and demands were offered but that they were only temporary. For him, abstinence and privation were the only answer and interpretations were to be the only therapeutic tool and source of gratification.

This technical advice was excellent and sufficient to help the majority of patients, but unfortunately there were patients, usually severely disturbed hysterics, who were not helped by privation and interpretation, at least as far as interpretative technique was understood in the twenties and thirties of this century. This will be discussed later. Patients who wanted various forms of gratification from the analyst, ranging from the most apparently innocent, such as a little extra time for a session, up to demands for the most blatant physical contact, responded, if they did not receive them, by becoming lifeless, despairing, or mildly psychotic, and could not be helped further. These reactions influenced Sandor Ferenczi in Budapest to think about these problems and resulted in numerous technical papers in the twenties and thirties of this century. He believed that what was being experienced by the patient in these abstinence situations was a replay, a re-enactment, of original traumatic experiences that the patient as a child had undergone at the hands of adults resulting in an under- or over-stimulation of the child, to which the adults had responded by a lack of involvement on their part, thus implicitly disclaiming all responsibility for their share of the traumatic situation. Ferenczi was suspicious of the benevolent, sympathetic, but neutral attitude of the analyst, who, by his setting and technique, had invited regression in the patient to experience longings and demands. The patient was faced by privation from the analyst, who offered interpretations and reconstructions of the original traumatic situation instead; this was experienced by the patient as the analyst himself not accepting his responsibility and involvement for the present emotional state of the patient but just remaining cold, detached, and intellectual; thus the original postulated adult reaction had been replayed in the present. Ferenczi regarded these analytic attitudes as part of the professional hypocrisy of the analyst and he tried numerous experiments in technique to try to reach his patients in a different way. He believed that the aim of therapy should be to help the patient to regress to the original traumatic situation, to assess the degree of tension the patient could tolerate while in this state, and to see if the patient could be kept at this level by positively responding to the regressed patient's cravings and needs.

It was this positive responding that caused the rift between Freud and Ferenczi. Freud maintained that it would prove impossible to satisfy every need of a regressed patient, that any improvement by doing so would only persist as long as the analyst was at the patient's beck and call, and that, even if improved, the patient would never be really independent. Ferenczi believed otherwise. He had experienced a number of successful analyses in which the regression had not been too severe, or, in Michael Balint's later terminology, the regression had been of a benign type. Although he had also experienced some cases of malignant regression, Balint's other type, he had felt sufficiently encouraged to continue experimenting along his own path.

Ferenczi had always been clinically adventurous and had acquired a reputation of being able to take on and treat cases that colleagues had failed with. He was an ardent believer in the effects of trauma in the pathogenesis of mental illness and, to quote from the editor's introduction to his *Clinical Diary* (1988),

> he draws parallels between the child traumatised by the hypocrisy of adults, as described in his 'Confusion of Tongues' paper, the mentally ill person traumatised by the hypocrisy of society, and the patient, whose trauma is revived and exacerbated by the professional hypocrisy and technical rigidity of the analyst. He described the process that takes place in people who are victims of overwhelming aggressive force: the victim, whose defences have broken down, abandons himself in order to survey the traumatic event from a great distance. From this vantage point he may be able to consider his aggressor as sick or mad, and may even try to care for and cure him. Like the child who can on occasion become the psychiatrist of his parents, or the analyst who conducts his own analysis through his patients.
>
> (Ferenczi 1988: xviii)

This diary of 1932, kept in the last nine months of his life, is a fascinating document of Ferenczi's technique and theorizing at that time. He believed that every technical rule could be abandoned if that was appropriate in the interests of cure. In the entry of 17 January, he described the development of his technique over the years. At first he had tried to obtain catharsis of traumatic experiences by regressive means but this had not necessarily worked, as his attitude had been professionally impersonal; he then tried to increase tension in the patient by what he called active therapy in forbidding the patient to perform certain actions but this hadn't worked; he then tried lowering the tension by encouraging relaxation but this didn't necessarily work; he then tried admitting to the patient what he was feeling during the sessions – that is, admitting his counter-transference feeling of pleasure, annoyance, anger, boredom, and so on. This helped somewhat in some patients, but it was not enough. This led him to his most extreme experiment, mutual analysis, in which both analyst and patient took turns in analysing the other in a systematic fashion either in double or alternating sessions. In this way, it was not only the patient regressing with the analyst, but also the analyst regressing with the patient. It soon became evident to him that this technique created immense problems, such as the patient's projection of her problems into the analyst's declared problems and so deflecting attention from herself, the impossibility of the analyst being completely open and sincere about his thoughts and feelings towards the patient without prejudicing the continuation of the analysis, the impossibility of revealing one patient's confidences to the analyst to another patient if free association is to be really free. All of these problems were noted by Ferenczi in his diary, and eventually he realized that this technique too would have to be given up.

We must also remember that Ferenczi was allowing himself physical contact with patients, kissing and being kissed by them, and it was to this that Freud wrote his letter of 31 December 1931 to Ferenczi, pointing out that the almost certain consequences for his successors if erotic behaviour were gratified in analysis as a part of technique would result 'in an enormous increase of interest in psychoanalysis among both analysts and patients'. As a consequence of his experiments and Freud's attitude towards him, formal regression in the interests of therapy developed a bad name and was dropped from the therapeutic armamentarium of most analysts. It took several years before people, particularly Michael Balint, the analyst and collaborator with Ferenczi, and Donald Winnicott, looked again at this issue to see what positive features could be extracted from these experiments. Balint and Winnicott were the foremost workers, although Margaret Little (1985, 1987), Masud Khan (1972), Christopher Bollas (1987), and Harold Stewart (1977, 1987) have further developed our understanding of these states.

Let us first turn to Donald Winnicott. His most important paper on this topic, 'Metapsychological and clinical aspects of regression within the psychoanalytical set-up' (1954), opens with the sentence, 'The study of the place of regression in analytic work is one of the tasks Freud left us to carry out and I think it is a subject for which this Society is ready.' He classified patients into three categories; first, there are those who operate as whole persons, whose difficulties are in the realm of interpersonal relationships, and who need the technique of classical analysis; second, are those in whom the wholeness of the personality can only just be taken for granted, where the analysis is of the stage of concern, or depressive position, where the analysis is that of mood and the survival of the analyst is an important management problem; third, are patients who have no secure personality structure, before the achievement of space-time unit status, where the analysis is very dependent on management. Regression is particularly important for this last group of patients, where illness is related to early environmental failure leading to the development of the false self organization.

106

He describes the sequence of events in treatment.

1 The provision of a setting that gives confidence.
2 Regression of the patient to dependence, with due sense of the risk involved.
3 The patient feeling a new sense of self, and the self hitherto hidden becoming surrendered to the total ego. A new progression of the individual processes which had stopped.
4 An unfreezing of an environmental failure situation.
5 From the new position of ego strength, anger related to the early environmental failure, felt in the present and expressed.
6 Return from regression to dependence, in orderly progress towards independence.
7 Instinctual needs and wishes becoming realizable with genuine vitality and vigour.
All this repeated again and again.

(Winnicott 1954: 287)

Winnicott regarded regression as regression to dependence. The reason for this is that he regarded the mother and her baby as an inseparable unit; there was no such thing as a baby, only a baby and its mother. Hence the environment, first the mother and her management, is essential to his conceptualizing. Dependence on the mother and her management, and in treatment, on the analyst and his technique, are inseparable from the patient's responses and behaviour, both fundamentally influencing the other. He further stressed the important fact that interpretations of whatever nature given during the regression can ruin the emerging processes, whereas the interpretative work that needs to be done after emergence from the regression is essential for the progress of the analysis.

Regression to dependence is not synonymous with the earlier-described cathartic abreaction of repressed experience as produced, for example, by hypnosis. The essential difference between regression in hypnosis and psychoanalysis is that the former results from a collusive relationship between patient and hypnotist, which must necessarily be unacknowledged and unexamined if the hypnotherapy is to continue as such. The latter, however, is a naturally occurring, spontaneous event, which is acknowledged, scrutinized, and examined to the maximum in the patient–analyst relationship. The difference is in the authenticity of the phenomenon. Similarly, regression in analysis is different from the technique of the corrective emotional experience as devised by Franz Alexander (1948). He suggested that the principle of corrective emotional experience is a consciously planned regulation of the therapist's own emotional responses to the patient's material in such a way as to counteract the harmful effects of the parental attitudes. These artificial states, although useful and helpful in cathartic psycho-therapies, have no place in psychoanalysis.

Margaret Little has written on her own analysis with Winnicott in two papers, 'Winnicott working in areas where psychotic anxieties predominate' and 'On the value of regression to dependence' (1985, 1987). Regression to dependence is 'a means by which areas where psychotic anxieties predominate can be explored, early experiences uncovered, and underlying delusional ideas recognised and resolved via the transference–counter-transference partnership ... in both positive and negative phases'. She described his management of her, how he would increase the length of sessions to one-and-a-half hours on a regular basis, and how he would hold her hands or her head for long periods when he felt this was appropriate. Many analysts would not necessarily agree with these management arrangements but the idea that it is the 'unthought known', to use Bollas's felicitous phrase, the past experience or perhaps the phantasy of the past experience, that needed to be experienced, is well conveyed. A quaint, rather artificial, situation is the picture given of patients having to queue up to go through a period of regression, as the experience was such a taxing one for the analyst.

Yet Winnicott also described less dramatic types of experience embraced by the concept of regression to dependence. In his paper 'Withdrawal and regression' (1954), he described a patient who did not clinically regress but went into momentary withdrawal states during sessions. If the analyst then understood the patient correctly and did so by a correct, well-timed interpretation, the withdrawal was converted into a situation in which the analyst was holding the patient and taking part in a relationship in which the patient was in some degree regressed and dependent. This gave the opportunity for correction of inadequate adaptation-to-need in the patient's own infancy management and this must obviously be a fairly regular happening in all well-conducted analyses.

We shall now turn to Michael Balint and his contribution to this topic, although I shall be considering his work in more detail in the next chapter. This culminated in 1968 in the publication of his book *The Basic Fault*, which has the subtitle 'Therapeutic aspects of regression'; this represented a distillation of his thinking and working on regression for a period of over forty years. He had seen after Ferenczi's death in 1933 that several of the patients whom Ferenczi had treated so heroically had broken down again, and this had made Balint wary in trying to assess the value of Ferenczi's techniques. However, some of the cases had done well, and this encouraged Balint to make a careful examination of the techniques used and their results to get a more realistic assessment of their value. In doing this he was gradually able to reach certain conclusions and concepts that I shall briefly describe, and these, like Winnicott's, are bound up with ideas on infant development and psychological functioning.

He did not accept Freud's theory of primary narcissism and instead put forward his own theory of primary object love. In this, a harmony exists between the infant and its environment, the feeding and holding mother, in which only the needs and desires of the infant matter, with the mother existing only to satisfy them and to have no demands of her own on the infant. As inevitably this primary love is frustrated, hate and sadism will arise in the infant as secondary phenomena, together with the production of the basic fault in the mind. This geological metaphor refers to the residual scars in the personality that have arisen from the infant's response to the traumatic discovery of frustration and separation from its primary object. He postulated the development from this of two pathological character structures, ocnophilia and philobatism. In ocnophilia, objects are felt as safe and comforting and the spaces between objects are unsafe and threatening; in philobatism, the reverse is the case, with the spaces being felt as safe and comforting and the objects, unsafe and threatening. In these ways, both Winnicott and Balint believed in the primacy of object relations and postulated the development of pathological character structures from the discrepancies between the individual and the environment.

However, it was Balint who particularly recognized the potential dangers and pitfalls of regression, the dangers that had resulted in the estrangement of Freud from Ferenczi. He differentiated two forms of regression, benign and malignant regression. The benign form, as its name implies, was thought to be harmless, the regression being in the interests of the patient trying to reach something within himself. The malignant form was the exact opposite of this, where patients wanted and demanded active gratification of their wishes from their therapist, a procedure which could very easily spiral into disastrous depths for the therapy. The differentiation of these states is not always easy, but is essential for the outcome of treatment. These issues will be illustrated and discussed in the next chapter.

To complete the topic of regression, I need to mention the work of Ernst Kris (1935). His interest in regression was mainly from the viewpoint of artistic creativity. He preceded Balint in differentiating two forms of regression, one form being characterized by the ego being overwhelmed by the regressive process, whereas in the other, the regression is in the service of the ego. These forms roughly coincide with Balint's malignant and benign regressions; Kris did not elaborate

on their clinical significance but used them in his theories of sublim-
ation and creativity.

In this overview of regression, I think it is clear that the advances in
this therapeutic agency have come about from the increased understanding of the underlying psychopathologies of patients and the
appropriate techniques for dealing with them. Ferenczi, in his time, did
not seem to have the understanding of the sheer malevolence of the
severely hysterical patient. He tended to be a therapeutic idealist who
believed in the supreme power of the uncovering, the re-living and
emotional understanding of early traumatic experiences, and was
convinced that the analyst, by his love, sympathy, and understanding
in a maternal stance, had to fit in with the patient completely in order
to avoid being experienced as the uninvolved, neutral, verbal observer.
He did not have the concept of envy of the good breast, the good and
helpful analyst, and the compulsive urge to destroy the very source of
help, love, and understanding; neither did he have the concept of
destructive narcissism. He did not appreciate that when the patient was
apparently responding favourably, it was often in a state of idealization
and denial. Similarly, the understanding of the analyst's inevitable
failures of the patient in many small ways, of the anger associated with
these failures, and of the analyst's acknowledgement of the failures was
insufficiently appreciated. We must not, however, forget the importance of the lead that Ferenczi gave us in the understanding and use of
the counter-transference and of the importance of the part played in
analysis by the analyst's technique and behaviour. We must also not
forget that in addition to the advances in interpretative technique that
I have just mentioned, therapeutic regression, where relevant and
properly handled and understood, remains an important therapeutic
technique in analysis.

9

Technique at the basic fault and regression[1]

We shall now examine Balint's work on therapeutic regression in more depth and, particularly, its clinical aspects and the technical problems that are encountered in working with regressed patients. He, like Winnicott, was sympathetic to many of the views of Melanie Klein, although neither considered themselves followers of her school. The concept of therapeutic regression is absent from the literature of both the Kleinians and Contemporary Freudians, but certain aspects of Kleinian theory are useful in thinking about the phenomena encountered in this area. So let us first turn to the idea of the basic fault and remind ourselves of Balint's thinking when he coined the term.

Like most other analysts, he noticed that although an analysis might have started and proceeded reasonably smoothly with both analyst and patient intelligibly understanding each other, at some point suddenly or insidiously the atmosphere of the analytic situation changed profoundly. The foremost change was that interpretations ceased to be experienced by the patient as such but rather as persecuting comments or as a seductive and gratifying statement. Common or garden words became highly charged positively or negatively and every gesture or movement of the analyst assumed great importance. Furthermore, the patient seemed able to get under the analyst's skin and apparently understand too much about the analyst in interpreting the analyst's behaviour with great accuracy but in a lopsided and out-of-proportion manner. The patient could even become telepathic or clairvoyant. A patient of mine knew it was my birthday although she had no way of knowing or finding this out; another knew that I had been left some money by a relative, even to knowing almost the correct amount. If the analyst failed to 'click-in', to use Balint's phrase, to respond as the patient expected him to do, there was often no reaction of anger, contempt, or criticism but a feeling of emptiness, deadness, and futility, coupled with an apparently lifeless acceptance of everything offered by the analyst. Sometimes persecutory feelings emerged, in that the patient thought that the analyst was behaving intensively maliciously towards him, although at the same time the patient showed unshakeable determination to get on with things in the analysis which made him very appealing to the analyst, a sign of positive counter-transference. The appearance of this total picture of a near-psychotic state indicated, according to Balint, that the level of the basic fault had been reached.

Why did he give it this name? First, Balint believed that the events described indicated that they were more elementary and primitive than those belonging to a three-person Oedipal psychology but belonged rather to the field of a two-person psychology, and, second, that the events lacked the dynamic structure of a conflict. Hence the use of the word 'basic'. The word 'fault' arose from the fact that this word was used by many patients to describe the state, as though there was a fault in their minds that had to be put right, since the cause of this fault was that someone had failed or defaulted on the patient. It was more akin to a geological term than a moral one. The anxieties in the analysis were that the analyst should not also fail the patient. Since the term 'basic fault' has readily been accepted into our analytic terminology, it must be that it touches on a basic resonance in the thinking of analysts. This psychic state is clearly akin to that of a transference psychosis but, as far as I know, no one, other than Balint, has included parapsychological phenomena in their descriptions of such states. No doubt, Freud, with his interest in the occult, would have been interested in Balint's observations.

The basic fault was then a manifestation of psychopathology and Balint had his own hypothesis or model of human development. He did not accept Freud's theory of primary narcissism and in the chapter in his book entitled 'Primary narcissism and primary love', he set out in detail the reasons for his objections. He believed in the concept of primary love, which is considered in detail in his book *Thrills and Regressions* (1959), but briefly he maintained that

> a healthy child and a healthy mother are so well adapted to each other that the same action inevitably brings gratification to both ... the theory assumes that there exists a harmony between the individual and his world; that is, there is not – and cannot be – any clash of interests between the two.
>
> (Balint 1959: 65–6)

At this stage of development there are as yet no objects, although there is already an individual, who is surrounded, almost floats, in substances without exact boundaries; the substances and the

112

individual mutually penetrate each other; that is, they live in a harmonious mix-up.

(p.67)

He compared this state with the water in a fish's gills or oxygen going into the lungs; was the water or oxygen outside or inside the organism? Equally the organism took the water or oxygen completely for granted, to be used without effort or thought. Balint maintained that hate and sadism were secondary to frustrations of the primary love relationship, rather than their being primary drives in their own right; in this, his theorizing is akin to that of Fairbairn.

Inevitably this ideal state of primary love could not last and it is here that the basic fault arose in the individual's response to the traumatic discovery of frustration and separation from its primary object. In his view,

> the origin of the basic fault may be traced back to a considerable discrepancy in the early formative phases of the individual between his bio-physiological needs and the material and psychological care, attention, and affection available during the relevant times. This creates a state of deficiency whose consequences and after-effects appear to be only partly reversible. The cause of this early discrepancy may be congenital ... or environmental, such as care that is insufficient, deficient, haphazard, over-anxious, over-protective, harsh, rigid, grossly inconsistent, incorrectly-timed, over-stimulating, or merely un-understanding or indifferent.
>
> (Balint 1968: 22)

The more the discrepancy, the more intense and pathological became the consequences for that individual.

Balint then suggested that there were two methods by which the individual might have responded to the trauma of this relationship with the primary object, which were distinct from the withdrawal of libidinal cathexis from the object back into the ego, which would have given rise to secondary narcissistic states. The first way entailed the cathexes adhering to the objects, making them feel safe and comforting, but having as a result that the spaces between the objects felt horrid and threatening; the second entailed the spaces between objects being experienced as safe and friendly, whereas objects were felt to be treacherous hazards. The first method he called 'ocnophilia' and the second, 'philobatism'. He noted the close relationship of these to the states of agoraphobia and claustrophobia, and in view of the fact that the borderline states and severe perversions have been recognized by analysts of differing theoretical orientations as having a pathology along

113

the claustrophobia–agoraphobia axis and the severe anxieties of merging and of separating, there does seem to be a general agreement concerning this type of basic pathology.

Let us now return to the patient who had regressed to the basic fault level as described by Balint and let me give an example. A patient in this phase experienced my customary way of ending a session as an expression of my hating her, of my picking on her, and of treating her very badly. She demanded to know why, if my wife and family lived in my house in which I practise, she had to leave my house, as she had as much right to be there as they did. She could see no difference between my relationship with my family and my relationship with her. Patients in this phase of an analysis may often expect full gratification of their needs and wishes by the analyst since they are often experienced as compulsive and concrete in nature, and the technical problems involved will be discussed later in the paper. Balint defined the problem as

> how to enable an uncooperative part of an individual to cooperate, that is, to receive analytic help ... to stimulating, or perhaps even to creating, a new willingness in the patient to accept reality and to live in it, a kind of reduction of his resentment, lifelessness, etc., which appear in his transference neurosis as obstinacy, awkwardness, stupidity, hypercriticism, touchiness, greed, extreme dependence, and so on.
>
> (1968: 88)

In my experience, this description is not strong enough, as it does not encompass the sheer malice, destructiveness, and extreme envy that is also behind the lack of cooperation. Khan (1969), in his essay on Balint's researches, had previously made this point as a result of his experience of working with these patients.

Before coming to technical considerations, we should look at Balint's views on the regressed state itself. He had continued, in spite of the atmosphere in the psychoanalytic world towards therapeutic regression following on Freud's open disagreement with Ferenczi's experiments, to allow patients in regressed states to gratify their needs for certain satisfactions in the analytic situation, the most extreme seeming to be touching or holding the analyst's hand. Gradually he began to think that such gratifications, given in what he called an *arglos* atmosphere, were not important in themselves but could be a way of freeing the patient from the complex rigid and oppressive compulsive forms of object relationships to which the patient had regressed. He defined *arglos* as 'a constellation in which an individual feels that nothing harmful in the environment is directed towards him and, at the

114

same time, nothing harmful in him is directed towards his environment' (1968: 135). It is comparable to basic trust. This state is an essential precondition for a 'new beginning' in the patient, which is 'the capacity for an unsuspicious, trusting, self-abandoned and relaxed object-relationship' (1952). The *arglos* atmosphere and 'new beginning' are clearly closely related to his concept of primary love. Balint then postulated that this form of regression is not an attempt on the patient's part to gratify an instinctual craving but rather a way of using the environment to enable him to reach himself; he called this 'benign regression' or 'regression aimed at recognition' (1968: 144). This concept is very close to Winnicott's ideas of ego-needs as against id-wishes and his dividing of the primary maternal figure into the environment-mother and the object-mother (Winnicott 1963).

However, we should note that in the near-psychotic state of the basic fault as described, the *arglos* atmosphere and its significance for new beginning could not exist. This is the realm of the other type of regression described by Balint, 'malignant regression' or 'regression aimed at gratification' (1968: 144). He noticed that patients had seemed to fall into two groups; in one the enactment of some form of simple gratification in the analysis where the atmosphere was an *arglos* one was sufficient to allow a satisfactory new beginning to occur. In the other, however, if there was any form of gratification and satisfaction of primitive wishes or needs, further demands for gratification were made and a constant spiral of urgent demands occurred, often leading to addiction-like states which were very difficult to handle. The atmosphere in these states was not *arglos* in the attempt to reach the self, but desperate, passionate, and of high intensity in the demands for gratification by external action on the part of the analyst — hence the name, 'malignant regression'. Balint noted that the clinical picture in these patients showed signs of severe hysteria. Ferenczi's treatment of these patients had often led to malignant states of regression, and his attempts to find ways and means of dealing with the spiralling demands had led to Freud's disagreement with these attempts. Nevertheless, Balint believed that Ferenczi's work in this area had led to two major discoveries. One concerned the effect of the analyst and his particular technique on the developing transference relationship; the other concerned the therapeutic possibilities of counter-transference interpretations (Balint 1968).

We now need to turn to the technical features and problems which arise when working at the basic fault level and see how Balint regarded them. He started from the observation that in some patients, where he believed that their compulsive patterns of behaviour and object relationships originated in a reaction to the basic fault, interpretations would have incomparably less power since (1) there was no conflict that needed to be resolved, and (2) words were no longer experienced as very reliable tools. He believed that in these cases additional therapeutic agents other than interpretations should be considered, and in his opinion,

> the most important of these is to help the patient to develop a primitive relationship in the analytic situation corresponding to his compulsive pattern and maintain it in undisturbed peace till he can discover the possibility of new forms of object relationship, experience them, and experiment with them ... a necessary task of the treatment is to inactivate the basic fault by creating conditions in which it can heal off.
>
> (Balint 1968: 166)

How does one foster this process in the analysis? Interestingly, Balint started by emphasizing three things that the analyst should try to avoid doing. The first was to avoid interpretating everything first as a manifestation of transference, which is one present fashion in interpretative technique. Balint thought that this style of interpretation 'tempts us to turn into mighty and knowledgeable objects for our patients, thus helping – or forcing – them to regress into an ocnophilic world' (1968 166). By this, I believe he meant the constant references to the overt patient–analyst relationship. In this way, independent discoveries by the patient about himself tended to be discouraged. I myself believe that by working only in the transference, the effect is to devalue all the patient's relationships with people other than the analyst, which forces the patient into the ocnophilic world of the analyst himself – that is, it can be a counter-transference manifestation in the original sense as used by Freud.

The second thing was 'not to become, or to behave as, a separate, sharply-contoured, object ... [but to] allow his patients to relate to, or exist with, him as if he were one of the primary substances' (1968: 167). By 'primary substances', he meant water, earth, air, and fire. In this way he seemed to be implying that the analyst tolerated some types of acting-out and that he also accepted the patient's transference projections and projective identifications without wanting to hurry to interpret them back into the patient. The third point was to avoid becoming or appearing to be omnipotent.

> This is one of the most difficult tasks in this period of the treatment. The regressed patient expects his analyst to know more, and to be more powerful; if nothing else, the analyst is expected to promise, either explicitly or by his behaviour, that he will help his patient out

116

of the regression, or see the patient through it. Any such promise, even the slightest appearance of a tacit agreement towards it, will create very great difficulties, almost insurmountable obstacles, for the analytic work.

(Balint 1968: 167)

He noted that several other analysts had described this sort of object relationship of being like an indestructible primary substance in their own particular terms; 'need-satisfying object' (A. Freud), 'average expectable environment' (Hartmann), 'container and contained' (Bion), 'good enough environment', 'ordinary devoted mother', 'medium', 'primary maternal preoccupation', 'holding function of mother', 'facilitating environment' (all these by Winnicott), 'basic unity' (Little), 'protective shield' (Khan), 'mediator of the environment' (Spitz), 'extra-uterine matrix' (Mahler).

Balint continued with his technical recommendations. He suggested that with patients regressed to the basic fault level, the analyst should bear with the regression without any forceful attempt at intervening with an interpretation, particularly those that are aimed at trying to get the patient out of the regressed state. The regression might have lasted for minutes or for many sessions but nevertheless it should have been borne with and tolerated as a mutual experience. He maintained that the analyst should accept the acting-out in the analytic situation as a valid means of communication and that it should not be speedily organized into understanding interpretations. He insisted, however, that this did not mean that the acting-out was not eventually to be understood by interpretative work with the patient, but that for the time being, the non-verbal communication had to be experienced in its own right and, only later, be put into organized verbal concepts.

These recommendations of accepting the experience of the regression and acting-out without speedy interpretative work, meant that the emphasis was placed on the mutual sharing of the experience in the analysis and that this is an important therapeutic agent in its own right and not simply as the vehicle for therapeutic, insightful interpretations. This emphasis, I believe, is one of the most important theoretical differences between the Independent on the one hand and the Kleinian and Contemporary Freudian groups on the other; it is, of course, a most important ingredient of Winnicott's theoretical position. In addition to this space for non-verbal experience, Balint stressed the importance of the provision of time and milieu:

What the analyst must provide − and, if at all possible, during the regular sessions only − is sufficient time free from extrinsic temptations, stimuli, and demands, including those originating from

117

himself (the analyst). The aim is that the patient should be able to find himself ... discover *his* way to the world of objects – and not be shown the 'right' way by some profound or correct interpretation.

(1968: 179–80)

He also held that

interpretations particularly should be scrutinized most meticulously, since they are felt more often than not as unwarranted demand, attack, criticism, seduction, or stimulation; they should be given only if the analyst is certain that the patient *needs* them, for at such times *not giving* them would be felt as unwarranted demand or stimulation.

(1968: 180)

This, to re-emphasize, is not to deny or denigrate the vital importance of interpretative work; it is to dispute its exclusive role as a therapeutic agent in analysis.

One effect of the excessive use of transference interpretations may well be that of the analyst unwittingly colluding with the ocnophilic, agoraphobic tendencies in the patient by stimulating and encouraging the mental clinging to the object, the analyst. Similarly, failure to offer such interpretations, if necessary, may collude with the philobatic, claustrophobic tendencies in the patient. This means that in practice there is a necessary delicate balance and fine judgement required to decide on the type and degree of interpretation given and on the amount of silence shown by the analyst towards the patient.

We should now look at some of the clinical examples that Balint gave to illustrate this aspect of the work at the basic fault level. I should say at once that his examples are all taken from patients in a state of benign regression and none from a state of malignant regression. There is no discussion of techniques that could be used for patients when they have regressed to this state but there are recommendations of how to try to prevent patients from regressing into a malignant state. I shall attempt to discuss technical issues concerning this state later in this chapter.

The first case described was the well-known one of the girl who did a somersault in the consulting room. She was in her late twenties and her main complaint was an inability to achieve anything. In the second year of her analysis in response to an interpretation, she said that since earliest childhood she had never been able to do a somersault. In response to Balint's comment, 'What about it now?', she got off the couch and did a perfect somersault; this led to a breakthrough and new beginning in terms of her treatment and personal life. He called this acting-out a regression since, although it was not a repetition of an actual early event, it was a repetition of a more primitive form of behaving and experiencing.

Another case was one of a woman whom he allowed to hold one of his fingers for some time during the analysis. He mentions this allowing of the finger- or hand-holding as part of his technique when he felt that the atmosphere was of the *arglos* type. Two further cases described were rather opposite in nature. The first was of a man who had to be on sick leave from work for several weeks during a new beginning period. He stayed in bed, came regularly to his sessions and asked for extra sessions especially at weekends, or that the analyst should telephone him, which he did. The second was of a man who, on Fridays, often asked for an extra weekend session and had been given them. This had not helped the analysis to progress, the patient being one who had always resisted real analytic contact. Eventually the analyst decided not to accede to the request for an extra session, giving the reason that to accede made the patient feel small and weak and the analyst seem all-powerful. The patient telephoned that evening to tell the analyst he was near to crying, and following this, some progress was made in the analysis. In the only other case given, a man who was in the second year of his analysis, was silent for about thirty minutes of the session and the analyst also remained silent, having previously had experience of the silence. On this occasion the patient had broken the silence by sobbing and then spoke of being able to reach himself. Since childhood he had not been left alone but had always had someone telling him what to do.

These cases illustrate the comparatively unobtrusive technique of the analyst and are no doubt familiar to most analysts from their technique although some of these examples would be controversial. The tacit encouragement given to the somersault patient, the finger- and hand-holding, and the telephoning of the patient show a more active technique that many of us would disagree with; one could say that this activity, perhaps acting-out, on the analyst's part is not easy to reconcile with the concept of unobtrusiveness although this could well be a matter of balance. Nevertheless, all the cases demonstrate some degree of acting-out by the patients which the analyst accepts, and they do seem then to be able to reach to something new in themselves which is beneficial to their therapeutic progress. Yet, interestingly, not all of the cases demonstrate a gratification of the patient's needs or wishes; the man who was refused the extra session was certainly not gratified in the usual sense of the word, yet the refusal was helpful to him. This represents a topic not discussed by Balint, which is crucial at times, and this is the importance of being able to say 'No', to frustrate the patient, when appropriate. It is a truism that a vital part of the analytic situation without which the analysis cannot succeed is the maintenance of the analytic setting and its boundaries. Some patients repeatedly test these boundaries to see the quality of the analyst's holding capacities; this is indeed one of the characteristics of a malignant regression. This maintaining of the setting and its boundaries may be described as an ego-need of the patient, which is crucial for the patient's gradual differentiation of self from others; the necessity for the analyst, as for the parent of a child, to say 'No' is an ego-need. The id-wishes for gratification of the patient are those to which the analyst must say 'No'. The problem for the analyst is to differentiate an ego-need which needs to be gratified by the analyst's acceptance from those where the gratification of the ego-need lies in saying 'No' to an id-wish. Balint had attempted to do this by the differentiation of the different atmospheres and intensity of desires in these two types of regression, but at least in one instance, he seemed to be underestimating the problem and this was in the context of physical contact between patient and analyst, even in finger-holding or hand-holding.

He thought that in the context of an *arglos* atmosphere, this physical contact is not only acceptable but therapeutically helpful, and his experience that it did not seem to be addictive must have encouraged him in this belief. It is very important here to note that Balint was very much against allowing physical contact of any sort except in this context. My own experience of him very firmly forbidding me to hold or allow any hand contact with my first supervised training case during the second year of her analysis bears this out. In this respect he differed considerably from Winnicott, and he indicated this gently in Chapter 18 of *The Basic Fault*. Strangely enough, Balint seemed to sound a warning against touching in his previous book *Thrills and Regressions*:

> I thought that the need to be near to the analyst, to touch or to cling to him, was one of the most characteristic features of primary love. Now I realise that the need to cling is a reaction to a trauma, an expression of, and a defence against, the fear of being dropped or abandoned.

> (1959: 99–100)

In the more recent literature, Casement (1982) gives a description of his patient's early traumatic experiences with her mother which emerged in the analysis when he refused to allow hand-holding; this confirms Balint's seeming warning. Pedder (1976) describes his experiences with a patient in which he allowed hand-holding and found it therapeutically helpful. Yet in a preface to this paper, published in *The British School of Psycho-Analysis: the Independent Tradition*, ten years later, he writes: 'The technique used has not become a standard part of my therapeutic repertoire, and I have not handled a case in a similar way since. Perhaps I now rely more on the interpretative mode' (pp.295–6). I have noted, and so have some colleagues, that after allowing hand- or finger-holding, even though it is late in the analysis and in an *arglos* atmosphere, the patient will have a dream, frightening or otherwise, of being raped or sexually assaulted. The inference is that the unconscious experience of the patient had been very different from that of an innocent physical contact. My last point concerning the wish or need for physical contact is that I have only experienced such requests from female patients and never from a male, but perhaps this may be because my experience of treating male homosexuals is relatively limited.

My conclusion from these points is that although physical contact may be therapeutically useful, it may also conceal more than it discloses. Furthermore, it also makes me wonder about the nature of the *arglos* atmosphere. It could well be that on some occasions the atmosphere may seem to have this quality because the psychic realities of persecutory traumatic and sexual anxieties have been split-off and denied, leaving the opposite state of innocence and guilelessness in a hysterical-type defensive manoeuvre. As the analyst cannot differentiate the real *arglos* state from the fraudulent, it seems therapeutically more advantageous to forgo physical contact rather than risk colluding with the patient's denials. The differentiation of the innocence and guilelessness of something genuine from that of a hysterical defensive manoeuvre would apply to all states of benign regression and not only to physical touching. During the regression, differentiation could be effected on the basis of one's counter-transference, if one were becoming bored, detached, or irritated. Otherwise it might be detected after the regression by a scanning of the material in the next session, perhaps of a dream, a parapraxis, or a counter-transference response.

I will give an example of a benign regression of one of my own patients, and part of its interest lies in the fact that it extended over more than a session. A borderline patient after a few years of analysis was associating on the couch on a Friday when the atmosphere suddenly changed and she felt that there was a dead man in the consulting room. She said she knew there wasn't one but felt as though he was there lying on the floor. She described him as a good man whose soul could not be at peace, nor could it go away until he had been buried. However, as only she seemed to know he was dead, no one else had buried him. I did no interpreting but only tried to clarify the situation being described. The session ended and she departed. When she returned on Monday, she told me that on Saturday she had gone to the local library, had photocopied the prayers for the dead that are usually recited at a burial, and had then gone to her local cemetery. She could not find a freshly dug grave and so she sat on a seat in a quiet, isolated part of the cemetery and recited the burial prayers, crying all the time. After that she felt much better, feeling that he had now been buried and something completed, and then she suddenly realized why she had so often been in very tearful states for no apparent reason during most of her life. We were then able to work on this experience of hers both in and out of the transference, and she strongly felt that it had been very important to her that I had not interpreted the possible transference meanings to her on the Friday as she felt that she would then have experienced me as not really listening to and being with her but rather as pushing my own interests and ways of looking at things.

The main dynamics of the experience of the regressed state that we worked on were these:

1 She was tormented by the belief that she could never recapture the experience of a relationship with a good father figure, which she had last had in early childhood. She had suffered prolonged separation from him and had thought that he was dead; on his return, he had changed and become emotionally distant and uninterested in her.

2 She had the conviction that I was cold and uninterested in her, too, and treated me accordingly. However, whenever she perceived me as not conforming to this picture, she disavowed her perceptions and destroyed my reality so that it should not interfere with her belief system.

3 She felt that I was being made to suffer torment by her treatment of me and that I was haunted by thoughts of having to continue working with her.

4 I was torturing and tormenting her by all breaks in treatment, including weekends, or if she felt that my mind was not totally on her.

5 The burial was a magical reparative ritual for the suffering caused, both to her external analytic father and her own internal father.

Interestingly enough, exactly a year later, we got an anniversary reaction. She felt that the man's bones had been disturbed and some were sticking up out of the ground, but then realized that, although she had felt it was real, she now both knew and felt that it was not so and could now smile at her previous beliefs about all this, knowing they were all phantasy, like a fairy story.

Before coming on to the issue of malignant regression, I do want to re-emphasize the vital feature of this work with regressed patients and that is the necessity of thorough interpretative work on the patient after they have emerged from the regressed state. Balint's examples do not illustrate this aspect, and this could lead to the notion that Balint is only concerned with acting out and not with the rigorous interpretative work of an analysis; this would be a great mistake in considering his technical recommendations for analysts.

As I mentioned earlier, Balint gave only a cursory look at malignant regression. Khan (1972), in his paper on such a case, thought that malignant regression was basically reactive to a dread of surrender to resourceless dependence in the analytic situation. He characterized the patients as coming from an over-protected environment in infancy and childhood, which did not allow for the aggressive behaviour that is essential to the crystallization of identity and separateness of selfhood in the child. He also noted the presence of severe destructive envy which spoiled and negated any indication that the analyst's work had been helpful to the patient. My own experience would support his views on dread of surrender and of destructive envy, but I found that some of my patients came not from over-protected environments but under-protected ones, where the parenting had been unpredictable, often violent, and associated with prolonged separations. They were all very severe hysterical personalities, as Balint had suggested, with an underlying borderline-psychotic psychopathology.

When we consider malignant regression in the analytic situation, we need to think, with Balint, of the contribution to the regression that comes from the analyst and his technique as much as the contribution from the psychopathology of the patient. He believed, as previously described in the paper, that the more the analyst's technique was suggestive of omniscience and omnipotence, the greater is the danger of malignant regression. In addition to this, I would say that interpretations in sexual terms concerning sexual phantasies and conflicts, if given early in the analysis or when the patient is regressed to the basic fault level, can easily lead to mental states of over-stimulation and over-excitement which may easily lead to severe acting-out in a malignant fashion. The third contribution the analyst can make to a malignant regression is to gratify the patient's wishes.

Can we know at an early stage, apart from the patient's history, of the potential for this type of regression? I will give an illustration. A patient in the first few months of analysis telephoned on a Friday evening in an agitated state to tell me how unhappy she felt about her last session and the weekend break. We spoke for a few minutes and she felt relieved. On Monday we discussed the call and the break, and things were quiet through the week but on Friday she telephoned again in an agitated state for a few words. I then knew that in her repeating her acting-out, I had a problem: if I spoke to her as she wanted, she would be calm for the weekend but would there be further demands? If I didn't comply she might become more agitated over the weekend or else act-out in some other way. I felt I wouldn't comply, but I pointed out that she was repeating her behaviour of the previous Friday and that I thought it better to discuss it with her on Monday. When she slammed her phone down, I knew what I was dealing with and, some weeks later, trouble started in earnest.

This leads us to the situation in analysis where the analyst's contribution to the regression is minimal and that of the patient maximal. The types of acting-out that can occur in these states are many, but I will confine myself to a consideration of the very considerable difficulties that arise when the patient is violent or destructive or when the patient does not want to leave at the end of the session. The patient I previously described under 'Problems of management' (Chapter 7) provides an excellent example of a malignant regression in her physical assaults upon me. My task in that situation was to function as a physical container of the attacks, as a maintainer of sanity and boundaries in the relationship, and as a maintainer of my interpretative stance as an analyst to provide understanding between attacks. As Winnicott wrote, 'In violence there is an attempt to reactivate firm holding' (1964).

The patient who had destroyed her previous therapies presented different problems. Almost from the beginning of her treatment she would get off the couch, bang around in my room, and shout obscenities at me, but she did not physically attack me. At the end of sessions, she slammed the doors as hard as she could, rushing out into the street still shouting obscenities about me. Interpretative work was useless with her and when I noticed that the paintwork on the doors and surrounds was being chipped, I decided that I would insist that she stop this damaging behaviour to my property or I would terminate treatment. My limit of violence had been reached. She stopped this behaviour by difficult self-control, even going to the length of tying her hands together with string around her wrists, rather like handcuffs, in order to control her violence, but now her behaviour changed in that she did not want to leave at the end of sessions. I eventually had again to threaten to stop treatment if she didn't leave in order to control this but, interestingly, she still did not understand why she should have to leave at the end of a session. She wanted to know why she had to leave my house, whereas my family, whose presence in the house she was aware of, did not have to leave (see above, page 114). Why was she any different from them? She was incapable of understanding any distinction between my family and herself, and it took quite a time before I realized how basic her difficulty in understanding things we tend to take for granted really was. It was not until I spelled out to her that I chose to have my family staying in the house and that

I did not choose to have her staying, that she was satisfied and understood what I was talking about, and after this we had no further trouble on this score. This would serve as an illustration of Balint's description of the phenomenology of the basic fault, where words lose their usual socially accepted meanings and overtones, resulting in a fracture of communication.

These issues concerning the maintenance of the analytic setting, particularly by the confrontation of the patient with the analyst's boundaries and limits, are complex in nature, but we should take a brief look at some of the theoretical ideas involved in them. Winnicott, as I previously mentioned, described violence as the patient's attempt to reactivate firm holding, and in several papers he wrote of the necessity of giving patients the opportunity for experiencing legitimate hatred towards the analyst. The maintenance of the setting most certainly provides such opportunities. Bion's concept of the container which acts to accept the patient's projections without retaliation but with understanding and firmness is relevant here. Little (1985), writing of her experience of analysis with Winnicott when she was in a psychotic state, thought that in the context of the delusional transference, also called the 'transference psychosis', there is an identification with the analyst whereby his prohibitions automatically become the patient's own prohibitions and that these joined up with some element of sanity in the patient. Ogden (1979), writing on projective identification, postulates that the patient projects the sane aspect of himself into the analyst since the patient's anxiety is that the destructive aspects of himself will annihilate the sane. The aim then is to protect this sanity by projecting it into the analyst to join with the analyst's sane aspects. Ogden thinks that the evidence for this is that the patient accepted, perhaps under duress, the analyst's boundaries and limits without completely destroying them and the analysis. I would like to add the notion that the analyst needs to have the firmness and strength to maintain the setting and that he should not confuse these qualities with sadistic cruelty, which might well undermine him by making him confusedly anxious and guilty about his own healthy aggression.

Frances Tustin (1988), in her work with autistic children, has written of the basic necessity of actively maintaining the boundaries and limits of the treatment setting if the therapeutic work is to progress. She is dealing with the autistic child directly, whereas I am dealing with the autistic–child aspect of the adult. These limits and boundaries are essential for the patient to be able to internalize and identify with in the psychic construction of their own self-boundaries, which are essential for the development of ego–strength and control.

To conclude, I would like to repeat that Michael Balint, whose views I have necessarily had to simplify, had always seen the positive therapeutic potentialities of regressed behaviour in our patients. The technical procedures that I have been discussing about both types of regression are valid in dealing with a very wide range of experience with our patients and not just those at the level of the basic fault.

Note

1 First version published in the *International Journal of Psycho-Analysis*, 1989, 70: 221–30.

10

Interpretation and other agents for psychic change[1]

The task of the psychoanalyst may be said to be that of enabling the patient to effect psychic change of a positive and permanent nature for the establishment of psychic growth, development, and integration. What we mean when we speak of psychic change, and try to conceptualize it, is a complex issue and will vary according to the theoretical viewpoints of the individual analyst, so I shall confine myself to three basic ideas. Briefly, the first is that of altering the relationships between the id, ego, and superego with the hope of expanding the influence of the ego and diminishing the strength of both the superego and the id. The second concerns the recovery of previously split-off parts of the self and their re-integration into the psyche; the third will consist of the changes in the relationship between internal and external objects in terms of the paranoid-schizoid and depressive positions (Klein 1946). All three will reflect in varying proportions different aspects of most analysts' thinking about psychic change.

Analysts will all agree, on the basis of their own individual analysis and their clinical experience with analytic patients, that the most important agent for producing this psychic change is the transference interpretation, and in an earlier chapter I set out a tentative classification of the various types of such interpretation. The examples given would make it seem that these interpretations in some way spring out in full formulation for the analyst to offer to the patient, yet clinically this is only very occasionally the case. Usually they are developed and offered piecemeal, often over a number of sessions, as the emotional states that are being expressed in the immediacy of the analytic relationship are gradually understood in relation to the verbal communications, until they can eventually be offered as a complete formulation. In this way, it is somewhat artificial to speak of interpretations or any other agents as the mediators of psychic change since they all usually arise gradually out of a complex matrix of interactions and not as complete and separate interventions. Nevertheless, since Freud, we do accept that this type of conceptualizing of agents, even if somewhat artificial, is essential and necessary for clarifications of complex clinical situations and is of the greatest help to the analyst in enabling him to keep his bearings and his ability to tolerate both confusion and the anxiety of not-knowing.

When we speak of psychic change, what are the phenomena that could be observed clinically that would indicate that real and permanent psychic change has occurred? I would suggest the following:

1 Changes in the nature of the impulses, affects, and attitudes towards objects, both internal and external.
2 Changes in the tolerance of impulses and affects, particularly anxiety, shame, and guilt.
3 Changes in the modes of mental functioning, such as the modes of thinking and dreaming.
4 Changes in dreams and dreaming in terms both of the dream content and the ways of experiencing dreams.
5 Changes in the experiencing of self in terms of realness, fullness, and wholeness.
6 Changes in the initial symptomatology, although this could also indicate false improvement.

Changes in any of these, provided that they are maintained, will indicate that some permanent change has occurred even if some slipping back occasionally happens, as is inevitable in analysis. Changes may also be only temporary and this can be misleading. For example, a flight into health may look like a permanent change in terms of the disappearance of the initial symptoms, but this would usually break down at some future date. Similarly we shall see further on that certain agents, such as prohibitions and confrontations, may be vitally necessary ingredients for the effecting of permanent change under certain specific clinical circumstances, but, if so, they are then functioning on a temporary, and not a permanent, basis for the purpose of effecting such change.

Let us turn first to the topic of transference interpretations. In the earlier chapter, I have given examples of the various types of such interpretations and these provide the clinical basis on which concepts concerning psychic change are formulated. James Strachey, in his influential paper, 'The nature of the therapeutic action of psycho-analysis' (1934), maintained that the action of a transference interpretation was to effect a diminution in the strength of the superego, and he described this as a mutative interpretation. In this process, the analyst interprets the patient's impulses towards the analyst in the here-and-now, together with the analyst's phantasized behaviour. For the interpretation to be successful, the patient would recognize the difference between his phantasy of the analyst's behaviour and the analyst's real behaviour from his experience of the analyst at that moment and over the course of the analysis. It means that the patient will recognize the difference between the archaic phantasy object and the real external object of the environment. This new picture of the object will enable the patient to reduce the strength of his projected id-impulses and so be able to introject a more benevolent object into his superego and thus mitigate its severity. The innumerable small changes effected by such interpretations gradually permanently modify the strength of the superego. I would add to Strachey's formulation that the efficacy of the mutative transference interpretation relies heavily on the patient's capacity for reality-testing to recognize this difference, and, if this is missing, different problems arise that will be discussed further on in the chapter.

The more empathic type of transference interpretation in which the analyst, for example, recognizes and acknowledges his previous failure to understand his patient's sensitivities and vulnerabilities also operates on the basis of reality-testing. The patient would have been enabled to recognize the difference between the analyst's real behaviour in acknowledging his failure and the phantasized archaic object behaviour. This gives rise to a change towards a more benevolent superego. In this chapter I want to put forward and substantiate the thesis that there are more roads to psychic change than Strachey's mutative interpretation.

Winnicott, in his paper 'The use of an object' (1969), takes the process a step further. He suggests that the projective identifications of the destructive aspects of the self are dealt with by the analyst by tolerating them and interpreting, when appropriate, and not by retaliating. In this way the analyst and his analytic functioning survive. The fiercer the attacks made by the patient, the more important and more difficult this survival becomes. The outcome eventually is the creation of the quality of externality of the object, which, instead of being projected and subjective, becomes accepted as objective and separate from oneself. Winnicott maintains that the objective reality of objects in infantile development arises from the operation of the destructive impulses; this is the opposite of the classical viewpoint that the destructive impulses arise from the frustrations and separations of objects. Following the emerging reality of the analyst, his introjection, as in the other models, will form the more benevolent superego.

Denis Carpy (1989) in a recent paper, 'Tolerating the counter-transference: a mutative process', discusses this in the light of the patient's projections and destructive attacks. He suggests that it is the inevitable partial acting-out of the counter-transference, which would include the way interpretations are given, that allows the patient to see that the analyst is being affected by what has been projected, is struggling to tolerate it, and to maintain his analytic stance without grossly acting-out. If this is successful, the patient will then re-introject the previous intolerable aspects of himself and also introject the capacity to tolerate them as he has observed in the analyst.

It is important to note that in these various explanations of the process of psychic change in transference terms, it is not simply the transference interpretations in themselves that are mutative. The analyst's non-verbal behaviour in his analytic functioning is of equal importance in the mutative process. When we come to consider further agents of change, this aspect of the analytic situation will often be seen to play an even more prominent role.

This leads us to a consideration of the other type of interpretation, the extra-transference interpretation, which is related to the patient's object relations and environment outside of the analytic situation, both in the present and the past. This topic has been relatively neglected in the analytic literature, which has rightly centred on the transference and transference interpretations, and one of the few exceptions to this neglect is the paper 'The position and value of extratransference interpretations' by Harold Blum (1983). To quote him:

> Transference is not the sole or whole focus of interpretation, or the only effective 'mutative' interpretation, or always the most significant interpretation. Extratransference interpretation has a position and value which is not simply ancillary, preparatory, and supplementary to transference interpretation. Transference analysis is essential, but extratransference interpretation, including genetic interpretation and reconstruction, is also necessary, complementary, and synergistic. . . . Analytic understanding should encompass the overlapping transference and extratransference spheres, fantasy and reality, past and present. A 'transference only' position is theoretically untenable and could lead to an artificial reduction of all associations and interpretations into a transference mould and to an idealized *folie-à-deux*.
>
> (Blum 1983: 615)

Furthermore, 'Extratransference interpretation is not necessarily non-transference, but it does not deal with the transference to the analyst' (p.591).

Strachey in his paper believed that although extra-transference interpretations are essential in analysis, they are not mutative and thus do not bring about permanent change; in this, he differs from Blum and others, such as Balint in *The Basic Fault*, who believe that they can, on occasions, be mutative.

I will give two examples to illustrate such changes. The first is given earlier in Chapter 4 on 'Inner space', where I described the case of the patient whose mother had been suicidal and the development of cancer had been inexplicably felt to keep her mother alive. My explanation to her – in effect, an extra-transference interpretation – of the effect of the potentially killing cancer alleviating her mother's suicidal feelings resulted in the permanent psychic changes of her feelings for her mother, of feeling far less greedy for food, and, most importantly, of her experience of her own inner space.

The second example concerns a psychotic male patient who in a session told me he had a picture of himself as a criminal sitting in the electric chair. He was silent for some time, so I said that he may feel like a criminal awaiting execution as yesterday he had been telling me how awful his mother was and how much he hated her. He then told me again how dominating, domineering, and hateful she was towards him and continued to rail against her for some time. Suddenly he stopped, put his hand to his head, said 'Oh, my God', and went silent for several minutes. He then said how terribly shocked he suddenly felt when he realized that his mother was not so awful; that he just had been unable to stand any ticking off from her and so had magnified her ticking off a thousand times in his mind and turned her into a horrible monster. This made him feel like a criminal. He stopped but soon went on. How dare she tick him off, this woman who was just his skivvy, who was there to do everything for the wonderful him as it reduced him to the level of an ordinary boy. In this last sentence, I could recognize that he was talking about himself in the interpretative terms that I might have used to him, and so I wondered to myself where I came into it. However, he now complained that this treatment was terrible because every time he really recognized something, he knew that he could not go back in his thinking and feeling to where he had been before. He was, in fact, complaining that permanent psychic change had occurred. At the end of the session he could hardly get off the couch and walk steadily as he felt so shocked. Thinking over the session later, I realized that my chair in the consulting room could be seen to resemble the electric chair in its shape, and so I believe that he was putting himself in my place, thinking in my terminology, probably feeling he was the criminal stealing my place and my mind, producing the shock of insight with its 'terrible' consequences like the electric chair.

Both of these examples demonstrate that patients can develop permanent psychic change without the agent being a mutative transference interpretation. The changes have been produced by extra-transference interpretations and the patient's own capacity for doing psychic work, having internalized the thinking processes of the analyst. The process of this psychic change is the result of the changed perception of the patient's archaic objects arising from their reality-testing, either by the analyst in the first example or by the patient in the second. In this way it differs from the change in transference interpretations where the change is in the perception of the reality of the analyst – that is, the patient's immediate external object. In the first example, the mother, who had been largely an idealized object for the patient, had been found to have a damaged and rather persecutory suicidal aspect that had been split off in the patient's mind, and the result of my interpretation in explaining the previously inexplicable had resulted in a healing of that split, so that the mother, instead of being separately persecutory or idealized, now became a more real, whole, suffering woman for whom the patient now felt depressive concern. In the second example, the mother was realized not to be the archaic persecutory monster object but a more whole, concerned woman in her care of him. In this way, the superego becomes less persecutory and more benevolent. The aspect of the process of change which is common to both transference and extra-transference interpretations is the patient's ability for reality-testing, either of external or internal perceptions.

Extra-transference interpretations which concern the environment and object relations of the patient's past are interlinked with the third therapeutic agent of reconstruction, or construction, as it used to be called. In this the analyst presents the patient with his inferences about a piece of the patient's early history that he may have forgotten or of which he had not seen the significance. Freud was very keen on reconstruction, not simply for its therapeutic value but also for the validation of psychoanalysis. Today, in view of the greater stress laid upon transference work in the here-and-now of the defensive manoeuvres of the ego, reconstruction has lost some of its therapeutic significance. Nevertheless, a reconstruction can still be effective in producing permanent psychic change, as the example of my patient with her suicidal mother illustrates. The suggestions that I had given to her were not only an example of an extra-transference interpretation but also a reconstruction of the patient's early history which had not previously made any sense to her.

The fourth agent of permanent psychic change is therapeutic regression, which we have already examined in the previous two chapters, and I want to give an illustration of the way this technique would differ from one relying solely on transference interpretative work. It comes from the paper on 'Psychoanalysis and freedom of thought' (1977) given by Hanna Segal in her inaugural lecture as the Freud Memorial Professor of Psychoanalysis at University College, London. She described a man who unconsciously had a deep hatred of thought processes and was obsessed with women's breasts. He reported a dream of a woman giving the breast to a baby, who, he thought, represented an aspect of himself. In the next session he started to think of his analyst's breasts, spoke of being mad about them, and that throughout his life he had always been sucking something. As he was talking he was getting more and more dreamy and remote. The analyst drew his attention to this and reminded him of the dream of the breast. He interrupted her angrily saying he did not want to be made to think but only wanted to suck; that when he had thoughts it meant he had nothing to suck. In this description, I think it would be agreed that the interpretation given was perfectly correct and that it drew something very important to the patient's attention. However, something different might have been done at the point in the session when the patient began to get dreamy and remote. Instead of making an interpretation, no matter how correct it was, the analyst might have remained still and silent to allow the patient to reach and explore for himself the experience of being in this state in the presence of an analyst who is not intervening with an interpretation, since this is experienced as a request for thinking about something instead of simply experiencing.

The patient might well be retreating into an idealized omnipotent phantasy of being a baby at the analyst's breasts, or of being at one with the breast, and perhaps the patient may remember nothing afterwards of his experience of the regressed state. But the essential feature is that the time for the analyst, who tolerates the regression, to explore and interpret the patient–analyst interaction and experiences concerning the regression, is after the patient had emerged from the regressed state in his own good time, without having been brought out of it by the analyst. Whereas the first analyst would see this form of regression only as a defence, the other would regard it not simply as a defence but also as an important pre-verbal communication of an early object relationship either real or phantasized, which needs to be experienced, usually repeatedly, and understood. This experiencing and sharing with the analyst, in addition to the verbal interpretative understanding, is the agent of permanent psychic change. Balint has described the analyst functioning in this way as the 'unobtrusive analyst'.

I want to give an example of a patient who experienced regressed states during her analysis but remembered nothing of them afterwards. A borderline addictive patient after some years of analysis started to go

133

to sleep for about ten to fifteen minutes in the middle of her sessions and, when she awoke, could remember nothing of her sleep state except that she had been deeply asleep. She never dreamed apparently during these regressions. I could find no theme to suggest why she might want to escape from the session or any theme to suggest what she might want to be escaping to. Whether it was defensive or communicative – and we certainly tried to explore the possibilities – it continued and, since I felt quite comfortable and relaxed in this situation, I stopped trying to investigate it and simply accepted it as a feature of the analysis that I did not understand. After a very long period of time, she told me one day that she knew that there was something in her mind about her being asleep but she did not know what it was. A few days later she awoke and told me that she felt most strange as it seemed to her as if she had had a dream and it felt as though it were something in her mouth. Later she discovered that the dream in her mouth felt like some sort of woollen material, like a blanket, and she remembered being put out in her pram as a very young child where she would sleep and she enjoyed that feeling. This sleep regression had been her escape from the present with me to an earlier, happier period in her life which she was re-experiencing with me on this primitive, non-verbal level. As an aside, this is an example of the concept of the dream being a transitional object, and one of the types of transitional phenomena.

It has been argued that if the analyst uses the technique of tolerating therapeutic regression, he is avoiding the interpreting of the immediate defensive transferential implications of the regression and is thereby colluding with the patient by avoiding, particularly, the immediacy of the negative transferential aspects. In answer one would agree that this loss of immediacy does occur, even though other things are gained, but more importantly, this issue of immediacy is not invariably of paramount importance in analysis. Modern technique, as it is practised by analysts of all theoretical orientations, includes the toleration and containment of the projected identifications of unwanted aspects of the patient's self, particularly the negative aspects, for very considerable periods of time before contemplating interpreting them back to the patient. This is regarded, not as a collusion of non-interpretation, but as a necessary and therapeutic technical procedure, whereas immediate interpretation would very often be non-productive and non-therapeutic, particularly if it had been made to deal with the analyst's anxiety of his relative ignorance of the transference relationship at that moment.

What can we understand about the underlying mechanism of the change that occurs in benign regression? There has been either the emergence of some form of primitive behaviour that allows the patient to recover lost or undeveloped aspects of himself, or else the emergence of some past traumatic or gratifying experience or phantasy that had been lost to the patient and can now be assimilated into the patient's on-going self-experience. The patient has been able to reach something in himself in the analyst's presence. As this process nearly always occurs more towards the end, rather than the beginning, of the analysis, it suggests that the superego, as a result of all the transference interpretative work, has become more benign and tolerant. This has allowed the development of a basic trust to occur between patient and analyst which enables some measure of de-differentiation of separateness to occur between them, between self and object, between me and not-me. This de-differentiation of separateness, a benign experience of fusion between external objects, in terms such as basic unity, primary love, and so on, is, at the same time, accompanied by a differentiation occurring in internal objects, allowing what had previously been undifferentiated, fused internal objects to defuse into separate entities. Some of these differentiated objects can then reach consciousness as rather persecutory memory- or self-experiences, and then be assimilated into the self in the now more depressively concerned analytic atmosphere.

Transference interpretations of all forms in their very formulation are always concerned with the you-and-me of patient and analyst, and hence are implicitly a vehicle for establishing separation and individuation between them. This implicit activity is one of the reasons why they run counter to the psychic direction of a benign regression, where benign fusion, and not separation, is the operative psychic process. In certain regressions, extra-transference interpretations, in their demand for thinking and hence separateness at that moment, will also be antithetical to the regressed state. In malignant regressions, however, where there is usually a pathological near-concrete fusion of projective identifications from the patient into the analyst, transference interpretations are absolutely essential in being the main vehicle for achieving the necessary separateness and autonomy to allow healthy psychic growth to occur.

Lastly I want to turn to the problems that arise in analysis where a block, an impasse, develops to the flow of the analytic process. In these situations the patient no longer responds to any form of transference–counter-transference interpretations, as psychic forces are in operation that are inimical to further progress. For progress to be resumed, something else seems to be necessary. I want to emphasize that, in the sort of situations I have in mind, the impasse has not arisen as a result of the analyst's errors or his lack of understanding of the situation; if it had, the understanding and acknowledgement of these errors or the understanding of that which had previously not been understood would have been sufficient to allow the analytic process to resume. I am speaking of situations where errors or lack of understanding have not been a prominent feature. Now it is at this point that controversy arises, since some analysts, who believe that the only agent of permanent psychic change is a correct transference interpretation, will maintain that the impasse persists because the situation has not been sufficiently understood and that the appropriate transference interpretation has not been given.

Is there any way we can decide between these two points of view? I have no absolute prescription for this but I would make two points. The first is that one can never disprove the claim that, if only one could find the right transference interpretation, the impasse would be overcome. Karl Popper certainly established this argument concerning falsification. The second point is that some analysts have learnt from experience that they might need to alter their technique in order to overcome an impasse. The most prominent example of such an analyst is Herbert Rosenfeld, the first analyst to treat a patient in a state of transference psychosis by transference interpretations alone. He gradually came to modify his views, thereby causing considerable controversy among some of his colleagues. In his paper on the treatment of borderline patients (1978), he discussed an impasse in a patient suffering from a transference psychosis, where the patient was not responding to transference interpretations and was about to terminate his treatment. Rosenfeld sat the patient up, encouraged him to go over his criticisms and grudges towards his analyst, and gave no interpretations, simply adopting an entirely receptive, empathic listening attitude towards him. The result was that the patient did not terminate but continued his analysis. In a private communication (1985), concerning a case presentation of a patient who had suffered severe early traumata and wanted to terminate his analysis, he wrote that 'these patients are extremely difficult to treat and in my experience there is a great deal of necessity for extratransference interpretations in order to cope with the problem'. It is small wonder that in his last book, *Impasse and Interpretation* (1987), he advocated flexibility in the analyst's technique.

I, with many other analysts, have long accepted that, in these critical situations in analysis, something other than a transference interpretation may be necessary to help the analysis survive. It seems that these are situations in which the psychotic aspect of the self has achieved dominance over the non-psychotic, resulting in the loss of contact with some aspects of reality and rationality. Since transference interpretations are addressed to the rational aspects of the self, they are no longer heard as such by the patient. Under these circumstances, problems arise in the analysis, one of which may be the development of an impasse, either acute or chronic in nature, for which some other types of intervention will be necessary. Rosenfeld has supplied two types of intervention, the looking at the reality of the analyst by the patient and the giving of extra-transference interpretations in order to try to prevent the patient from terminating treatment. I therefore propose to regard this type of impasse under two headings: the first is of the type described above where the analytic situation has become intolerable *to the patient* and he is proposing to deal with this by ending treatment. The second heading is where the situation has become intolerable *to the analyst* and he is driven to find some way out of it as a last resort in order to prevent himself from stopping the treatment. It is this second situation that I now wish to discuss.

It is not unusual for the analyst to feel that a patient is becoming rather intolerable in his behaviour during sessions, but usually this can be dealt with by interpretative work and the episodes pass. The problem becomes acute when interpretative work is no longer effective and then the rather intolerable becomes intensely intolerable. I have already mentioned why I do not agree with analysts who put the responsibility for this situation on the failure of the analyst to understand and produce the correct interpretation, so what does in fact happen in these situations? Nina Coltart (1977) described the analysis of a depressed man who during the course of his analysis developed a prolonged profound silence, hateful and despairing in its quality to a psychotic degree, which did not respond in the slightest to anything she said. After a considerable length of time, she, one day, found herself becoming furious and bawled him out for his prolonged attack on her and shouted that she wasn't going to stand it for a second longer. This outburst lifted the impasse and changed the course of the analysis.

I have myself had a similar experience with a schizophrenic patient who also became silent, as though dead, during his analysis. I found myself over the months coming to hate this patient and developed the most intense murderous phantasies towards him. I knew that death was contained in the silence but no matter how I tried to interpret on the basis of my counter-transference and knowledge of his very traumatic past history, nothing changed. Eventually, after many months, I could stand it no longer and so I told him that I was feeling so murderous with his silence that I could no longer stand it, and that if he didn't start to speak by the end of the week, I would end his analysis. I suggested that he might then look elsewhere for someone who would understand and tolerate him better than myself.

137

This confrontation, or threat, as with Coltart's, also produced a profound effect on the analysis, but it was not until the anniversary of this confrontation that he told me about the silence. He had felt dead and wanted to be dead, and the only thing that could bring him back to life was for me genuinely to insist that I wanted him to live. My interpretations during his silence had been somewhere at times along these lines but it was only the actual confrontation and threat about his silence that afforded him the proof that this was what I genuinely wanted, and then he could start to live again. Something more than an interpretation was required to be the agent of psychic change in these patients. I can only conjecture on the nature of the dynamics of this procedure. It may be that the patient was in the grip of an extreme self-destructive process which could only be counteracted by a genuine show of angry threats, signifying care and concern for the patient by the analyst. This would have reinforced any feelings of concern and trust that had been formed by the earlier analytic work. It may be that this was a repetition of some early experience that was being enacted in the transference. I cannot account for why I acted in this way at this particular moment; I only know that my counter-transference feelings were of this overwhelming nature, and analytic understanding was no longer functioning in me at that moment.

I have also described in previous chapters the severe violent and destructive acting-out that may occur in severe borderline hysterical patients in a state of malignant regression. One could say that in these situations where the analyst finds the patient's behaviour is becoming intolerable, the analyst has to behave as a sane, rational person towards the rather insane, irrational patient. The analyst's is the only voice of sanity and control, and on the patient's ability to hear, listen to, and identify with this voice depends the future of the analysis. This sanity, of course, is also conveyed by an interpretation in most instances, but here the patient may be forcing the analyst to act out a role, other than that of being an interpreting analyst, to convince the patient that the analyst is genuinely and aggressively determined to maintain his own self-boundaries by setting limits to the patient's behaviour. This is the something that these patients need for them to be able to identify with in the psychic construction of their own self-boundaries, so necessary for the development of ego strength and control. These are examples of what Symington (1983) described as the analyst's inner act of freedom which causes a therapeutic shift in the patient.

This is a temporary, not a permanent, psychic change, and is not therapeutic in itself, but nevertheless it is essential for the creation of the necessary state of mind to achieve a sufficient degree of therapeutic alliance to allow those agents, such as interpretation, and so on, to operate for the production of permanent change. It could also be said that this violent and destructive behaviour has its positive aspect if we remember Winnicott's view that it is the destructive impulse and its containment that creates the reality of the analyst and his differentiation from the persecutory archaic objects.

To summarize, the agents for psychic change described are:

1 the various types of transference interpretations;
2 extra-transference interpretations;
3 reconstructions;
4 therapeutic regression;
5 techniques, other than interpretation, to overcome analytic impasse.

In a recent paper, Tom Hayley (1990) has written that charismatic influence or suggestion is an important factor in effecting psychic change as it is inherent in the five agents listed above. There is some truth in this, but I believe that this effect is minimal for the following reason. Hypnosis, the most powerful of suggestive techniques, is destroyed if the negative transferential aspects of the relationship are analysed, as I have described in Chapter 1, and so I believe that the suggestive elements in all procedures will also be reduced to the minimum if these transferential aspects are analysed. Transference analysis is the enemy of suggestion.

Conclusion

I have tried to summarize the technical procedures used to effect psychic change, albeit with the sometimes oversimplified clarity that is necessary for a comprehensible description of complex phenomena. If they are used with an overall flexibility, I and other analysts have found them therapeutically effective. I have stressed the concept of therapeutic regression, used in the circumstances and with the safeguards that I have described. This has led me to take the view that not everything psychotherapeutic can be laid at the door of the immediate verbal, interpretative understanding of conflicts and defences. I find that the non-verbal and pre-verbal aspects of early experiences and phantasies also need expressing, and sometimes this can only occur in a regressed state; the verbal understanding and interpretation will follow.

It is now being increasingly recognized that the actual nature of the primary objects is of vital importance to the developing infant. The infant, for example, will interact very differently with a severely depressed or psychotic mother than it would with a healthy mother, and the effect on the infant's developing intrapsychic structuring and functioning will be correspondingly different. The nature of the object is as important as, and perhaps at times more important than, the nature of the infant's own constitutional drives and phantasy systems in determining the nature of the infant's psyche.

The objective studies of infant–parent interaction are increasingly of importance to psychoanalysis, and they are particularly valuable when they can throw objective light on the various theoretical surmises of infantile psychic development that have been constructed from the subjective experiences of patients in analysis. Much of this experience will be pre-verbal and non-verbal in nature, and regressive experiences may provide further opportunities for the understanding of these early developmental states. It is for its therapeutic, and potential scientific, use that regression is of positive value in psychoanalysis.

Note

1 First version published in the *International Journal of Psycho-Analysis*, 1990, 71: 61–70.

Bibliography

Alexander, F. (1948) *Fundamentals of Psychoanalysis*, New York: W.W. Norton.

Balint, M. (1952) 'New beginning and the paranoid and the depressive syndromes', in *Primary Love and Psychoanalytic Technique*, London: Hogarth Press.

———— (1959) 'Regression in the analytic situation', in *Thrills and Regressions*, London: Hogarth Press.

———— (1968) *The Basic Fault*, London: Tavistock Publications.

Bick, E. (1968) 'The experience of the skin in early object relations', *International Journal of Psycho-Analysis*, 49: 558–66.

Bion, W.R. (1957) 'The differentiation of the psychotic from the non-psychotic part of the personality', *International Journal of Psycho-Analysis*, 38: 266–75.

———— (1958) 'On hallucination', *International Journal of Psycho-Analysis*, 39: 144–6.

———— (1962) 'A theory of thinking', *International Journal of Psycho-Analysis*, 43: 306–10.

———— (1967) *Second Thoughts*, London: Heinemann.

Blum, H.P. (1983) 'The position and value of extratransference interpretations', *Journal of the American Psychoanalytic Association*, 31: 587–617.

Bollas, C. (1987) *The Shadow of the Object*, London: Free Association Books.

Brenman, M., Gill, M. and Knight, R.P.P. (1952) 'Spontaneous fluctuations in depth of hypnosis and their implication for ego-function', *International Journal of Psycho-Analysis*, 33: 22–33.

Breuer, J. and Freud, S. (1895) *Studies on Hysteria*, SE 2.

Carpy, D.V. (1989) 'Tolerating the countertransference: a mutative process', *International Journal of Psycho-Analysis*, 70: 287–94.

Casement, P.J. (1982) 'Some pressures on the analyst for physical contact during the reliving of an early trauma', in G. Kohon (ed.), *The British School of Psychoanalysis: the Independent Tradition*, London: Free Association Books.

Coltart, N. (1977) 'Slouching towards Bethlehem ... or thinking the unthinkable in psychoanalysis', in G. Kohon (ed.), *The British School of Psychoanalysis: the Independent Tradition*, London: Free Association Books.

Devereux, G. (1953) 'Why Oedipus killed Laius', *International Journal of Psycho-Analysis*, 34: 132–41.

Eissler, K. (1953) 'The effect of the structure of the ego on psychoanalytic technique', *Journal of the American Psychoanalytic Association*, 1: 104.

Encyclopaedia of Religion and Ethics (1927) (ed. Hastings), 'Burial Customs', Edinburgh: Clark.

Ferenczi, S. (1909) 'Introjection and transference', in M. Balint (ed.), *First Contributions to Psychoanalysis*, London: Hogarth Press (1952).

——— (1955) Chapters 7, 8, 10, 11 and 13 in M. Balint (ed.), *Final Contributions to the Problems and Methods of Psychoanalysis*, London: Hogarth Press.

——— (1988) *Clinical Diary*, J. Dupont (ed.), Cambridge, Mass: Harvard University Press.

Frazer, Sir J. (1932) 'The influence of the sexes on vegetation', in *The Golden Bough: the Magic Art*, vol. 2, London, Macmillan.

Freud, S. (1895) 'Project for a scientific psychology', *Standard Edition of the Complete Psychological Works of Sigmund Freud* (SE) 1.

——— (1900) *The Interpretation of Dreams*, SE 5.

——— (1905) *Three Essays on the Theory of Sexuality*, SE 7.

——— (1915) 'The unconscious', SE 14.

——— (1921) *Group Psychology and the Analysis of the Ego*, SE 18.

——— (1923) *The Ego and the Id*, SE 19.

——— (1925) 'Negation', SE 19.

——— (1937) 'Constructions in analysis', SE 23.

Graves, R. (1955) *The Greek Myths*, vol. 2, Harmondsworth: Penguin Books.

Gill, M. and Brenman, M. (1959) *Hypnosis and Related States*, New York: International Universities Press.

Grotstein, J.S. (1978) 'Inner space: its dimensions and its coordinates', *International Journal of Psycho-Analysis*, 59: 55–61.

Hayley, T. (1990) 'Charisma, suggestion, psychoanalysis, medicine-men and metaphor', *International Review of Psycho-Analysis*, 17: 1–10.

Heimann, P. (1950) 'On countertransference', *International Journal of Psycho-Analysis*, 33: 81–4.

——— (1956) 'Dynamics of transference interpretations', *International Journal of Psycho-Analysis*, 37: 303–10.

Hughes, A. (1976) 'The use of dreams in the analysis of a borderline patient', unpublished.

Jones, E. (1923) 'The nature of auto-suggestion', *British Journal Medical Psychology*, 3: 206–12.

Joseph, B. (1985) 'Transference: the total situation', *International Journal of Psycho-Analysis*, 66: 447–54.

Kanzer, M. (1950) 'The Oedipus trilogy', *Psychoanalytic Quarterly*, 19.

Kernberg, O. (1975) 'The subjective experience of emptiness', in *Borderline Conditions and Pathological Narcissism*, New York: Jason Aronson.

Khan, M.M.R. (1969) 'On the clinical provision of frustrations, recognitions and failures in the analytic situation', *International Journal of Psycho-Analysis*, 50: 237–48.

—— (1972) 'Dread of surrender to resourceless dependence in the analytic situation', *International Journal of Psycho-Analysis*, 53: 225–30.

—— (1974) 'The use and abuse of dream in psychic experience', in *The privacy of Self*, London: Hogarth Press.

—— (1976) 'The changing uses of dreams in psychoanalytic practice', *International Journal of Psycho-Analysis*, 57: 325–30.

King, P.M.H. (1971) 'The therapist–patient relationship', *Journal of Analytical Psychology*, 18: 1–8.

Klein, M. (1946) 'Notes on some schizoid mechanisms', *International Journal of Psycho-Analysis*, 27: 99–110.

Kohut, H. (1971) *The Analysis of the Self*, New York: International Universities Press.

Kris, E. (1935) 'The psychology of caricature in *Psychoanalytic Exploration in Art*, New York: International Universities Press (1952).

Kubie, L.S. and Margolin, S. (1944) 'The process of hypnotism and the nature of the hypnotic state', *American Journal of Psychiatry*, 100: 611–22.

Laplanche, J. (reporter) (1974) Panel on 'Hysteria today', *International Journal of Psycho-Analysis*, 55: 459–69.

Lewin, B.D. (1946) 'Sleep, the mouth, and the dream screen', *Psychoanalytic Quarterly*, 15: 419–34.

Limentani, A. (1979) 'The significance of transsexualism in relation to some basic psychoanalytic concepts', *International Review of Psycho-Analysis*, 6: 139–53.

Little, M.I. (1981) *Transference Neurosis and Transference Psychosis: Towards Basic Unity*, New York: Jason Aronson.

—— (1985) 'Winnicott working in areas where psychotic anxieties predominate: a personal record', *Free Associations*, 3: 9–42.

—— (1987) 'On the value of regression to dependence', *Free Associations*, 10: 7–22.

Milner, M. (1969) *The Hands of the Living God*, London: Hogarth.

Monchaux, C. de (1978) 'Dreaming and the organizing function of the ego', *International Journal of Psycho-Analysis*, 59: 443–53.

Ogden, T. (1979) 'On projective identification', *International Journal of Psycho-Analysis*, 60: 357–74.

Pedder, J.R. (1976) 'Attachment and new beginning: some links between the work of Michael Balint and John Bowlby', in G. Kohon (ed.), *The British School of Psychoanalysis: the Independent Tradition*, London: Free Association Books

Raglan, Lord (1933) *Jocasta's Crime*, London: Methuen.

Rosenfeld, H. (1972) 'A critical appreciation of James Strachey's paper on the nature of the therapeutic action of psychoanalysis', *International Journal of Psycho-Analysis*, 53: 455–62.

—— (1978) 'Notes on the psychopathology and psychoanalytic treatment of some borderline patients', *International Journal of Psycho-Analysis*, 59: 215–21.

—— (1985) Private communication.

—— (1987) *Impasse and Interpretation*, London and New York: Tavistock; in association with the Institute of Psycho-Analysis. The New Library of Psychoanalysis, No. 1.

Rycroft, C. (1951) 'A contribution to the study of the dream screen', in *Imagination and Reality*, London: Hogarth Press, 1968.

—— (1968) *A Critical Dictionary of Psychoanalysis*, London: Nelson.

Sandler, J., Dare, C. and Holder, A. (1973) *The Patient and the Analyst*, New York: International Universities Press.

Schilder, P. (1922) 'Über das Wesen der hypnose', Berlin: Springer; English translation in *The Nature of hypnosis, Part 1* (1956) New York: International Universities Press, pp.7–41.

Segal, H. (1957) 'Notes on symbol formation', *International Journal of Psycho-Analysis*, 38: 391–7.

—— (1973) 'Atypical dreams', unpublished, in Scientific Bulletin of the British Psycho-Analytical Society.

—— (1973) 'Function of dreams', in *The Work of Hanna Segal*, New York: Jason Aronson, 1981.

—— (1977) 'Psychoanalysis and freedom of thought', in *The Work of Hanna Segal*, New York: Jason Aronson, 1981.

Sheppard, E. and Saul, L.L. (1958) 'An approach to a systematic study of ego function', *Psychoanalytic Quarterly*, 27: 237–45.

Singer, M. (1977) 'The experience of emptiness in narcissistic and borderline states: I and II', *International Review of Psycho-Analysis*, 4: 459–79.

Sophocles (1947) *The Theban Plays – King Oedipus*, Harmondsworth: Penguin Books.

Stewart, H. (1961) 'Jocasta's crimes', *International Journal of Psycho-Analysis*, 42: 424–30.

—— (1963) 'A comment on the psychodynamics of the hypnotic state', *International Journal of Psycho-Analysis*, 44: 372–4.

—— (1966) 'On consciousness, negative hallucinations, and the hypnotic state', *International Journal of Psycho-Analysis*, 47: 50–3.

—— (1968) 'Levels of experience of thinking', *International Journal of Psycho-Analysis*, 49: 709–11.

—— (1969) 'The nature of the controlling forces in the hypnotic relationship', in L. Chertok (ed.) *Psychophysiological Mechanisms of Hypnosis*, Berlin: Springer Verlag.

———— (1973) 'The experiencing of the dream and the transference', *International Journal of Psycho-Analysis*, 54: 345–7.

———— (1977) 'Problems of management in the analysis of a hallucinating hysteric', in G. Kohon (ed.), *The British School of Psychoanalysis: the Independent Tradition*, London: Free Association Books, 1986.

———— (1981) 'The technical use, and experiencing, of dreams', *International Journal of Psycho-Analysis*, 62: 301–7.

———— (1985) 'Changes of inner space', *International Journal of Psycho-Analysis*, 66: 255–64.

———— (1987) 'Varieties of transference interpretations: an object-relations view', *International Journal of Psycho-Analysis*, 68: 197–205.

———— (1989) 'Technique at the basic fault: regression', *International Journal of Psycho-Analysis*, 70: 221–30.

———— (1990) 'Interpretation and other agents for psychic change', *International Review of Psycho-Analysis*, 71: 61–70.

Strachey, J. (1934) 'The nature of the therapeutic action of psychoanalysis', *International Journal of Psycho-Analysis*, 50: 275–92.

Symington, N. (1983) 'The analyst's act of freedom as agent of therapeutic change', in G. Kohon (ed.), *The British School of Psychoanalysis: the Independent Tradition*, London: Free Association Books, 1986.

Tustin, F. (1988) 'Psychotherapy with children who cannot play', *International Review of Psycho-Analysis*, 15: 93–106.

van der Sterren, H.A. (1952) 'The King Oedipus of Sophocles', *International Journal of Psycho-Analysis*, 33: 343–50.

Winnicott, D.W. (1954) 'Withdrawal and regression' and 'Metapsychological and clinical aspects of regression within the psychoanalytical set-up', in *Collected Papers. Through Paediatrics to Psychoanalysis*, London: Tavistock Publications, 1958.

———— (1963) 'The development of the capacity for concern', in *The Maturational Process and the Facilitating Environment*, London: Hogarth Press.

———— (1964) 'Youths will not sleep', in C. Winnicott *et al.* (ed.) *Deprivation and Delinquency*, London: Tavistock.

———— (1969) 'The use of an object', *International Journal of Psycho-Analysis*, 50: 711–16.

———— (1971) *Playing and Reality*, London: Tavistock.

———— (1974) 'Fear of breakdown', *International Review of Psycho-Analysis*, 1: 103–7.

Wolberg, L.R. (1945) *Hypnoanalysis*, New York: Grune and Stratton.

Zetzel, E. (1968) 'The so-called good hysteric', *International Journal of Psycho-Analysis*, 49: 256.

Name index

Alexander, F. 107

Balint, M. xi, 1, 3, 4, 44, 80, 104–6
    passim, 111–23 passim, 126, 131
Bernheim, H. 14
Bick, E. 53
Bion, W.R. x, 3, 15, 34, 41, 59–62
    passim, 90, 117, 125
Blum, H.P. 130
Bollas, C. 106
Brenman, M. 9–10
Breuer, J. 8, 14, 102, 103

Carpy, D.V. 129
Casement, P.J. 120
Coltart, N. 137

Devereux, G. 18, 24

Eissler, K. 82

Fairbairn, W.R.D. 113
Ferenczi, S. 4, 8, 11, 104–6, 108, 110,
    115
Frazer, Sir J. 27–8
Freud, A. 117
Freud, S. 4, 8, 9, 14, 15, 57–9 passim,
    62, 90, 101–3 passim, 106, 132

Gill, M. 9–10
Graves, R. 24, 26, 27
Grotstein, J.S. 41, 52–3

Hartmann, H. 117
Hayley, T. 139
Heimann, P. 10, 18, 69–70
Hughes, A. 36

Jackson, H. 101–2
Jones, E. 9
Joseph, B. 98

Kanzer, M. 18
Kernberg, O. 42, 44, 54
Khan, M.M.R. 34–5, 41, 98, 106, 114,
    117, 123
King, P. 70–1
Klein, M. 111, 127
Knight, R.P.P. 9–10
Kohut, H. 75, 94
Kris, E. 109
Kubie, L.S. 9

Laplanche, J. 84
Lewin, B.D. 34
Limentani, A. 36–7
Little, M.I. 106, 107, 117

Mahler, M.S. 117
Margolin, S. 9
Mason, A.A. 7
Milner, M. x, xi, 41, 50–2, 88
Monchaux, C. de 36

Ogden, T. 125

Pedder, J.R. 120–1
Popper, K. 136

Raglan, Lord 26, 27
Rank, O. 24
Reich, W. 71
Rosenfeld, H. 80, 136, 137
Rowley, J. 1
Rycroft, C. 34, 67, 82

146

Subject index

acting-out 103; patient's physical 85–6, 98; regressive 118–19, 124, 138; toleration of 116, 117
agoraphobia 113–14, 118
alpha-function 61
analyst: anxiety of not-knowing 128; contribution of to malignant regression 123; empathy of 77, 136; holding capacity of 120; as holding/containing object 34, 118; and impasse in analysis 137–9; inner act of freedom of 138; non-verbal behaviour of 130; omnipotence of 116, 123; –patient collusion 98, 121; –patient relationship 68–9, 74, 117; separateness from 53; 'unobtrusive' 80, 119, 133; see also counter-transference; interpretation
anxiety: ego-overwhelming dreams 33–40 passim; in the hypnotic state 12, 17; of merging and separating 114; transference interpretation and 74, 76
arglos atmosphere (Balint) 114–15, 119, 121
atmosphere in analysis 78; *arglos* (Balint) 114–15, 119, 121
autism: boundaries in treating 125

basic fault 109, 111–26 passim; clinical material 114; indicators of the 111–12; and object relationships 114, 115; origin of the 113; origin of term 112; parapsychology in the 111, 112
beta-elements 61
bizarre object 15; in schizophrenia 59
blocks in analysis, see impasse in analysis

borderline states xi, 113–14, 138; clinical material 84–97
boundaries of analysis 120, 125; and autism 125; see also 'parameters' of analysis
breast: denial of hostility towards 34; development of thinking and 60–2; dream-screen and the 34, 35; obsession with 133

character analysis (Reich) 71
character structure (pathological) 109
claustrophobia 113–14, 118
clinical material: basic-fault 114, 118–25 passim; borderline hysteria 84–97; chronic schizophrenia simplex 58–63 passim; dreams 30–3, 36–9, 72; experience of inner space 42–51, 54–5; extra-transference interpretation 132–3; impasse in analysis 137–8; Lucy R. 14; transference interpretation 71–81 passim
collusion x, 2; analyst–patient 98, 121; in hypnotic state 11–14 passim, 17; between Oedipus and Jocasta 25, 29; transference (non-) interpretation as 118
communication in analysis 82–100 passim; analyst–patient xi; clinical material 84–97; non-(pre-)verbal 46–7, 99–100, 117–18, 133, 134, 139, 140; patient's drawings 88–9, 98; physical 85–6, 98
consciousness: and the hypnotic state 14–15; and thinking 57–61 passim
containment: by analyst 34, 118, 120,

148